"Erica Willis is not only a fantastic writer and speaker, but she's also the picture of encouragement and inspiration. Her irresistible energy, combined with relatable humor and a genuine passion for Jesus, draws the reader in to both her story and the incredible story God has written for each of us."

Mary Carver, co-author, *Choose Joy: Finding Hope and Purpose When Life Hurts*

"Erica's fun and witty way of sharing God's revelation in her life is compelling in an I-can't-put-it-down kind of way. Her increasing understanding and experience with the Holy Spirit will challenge and encourage you. Don't miss out. There is so much more to God than we think."

Janet McMahon, church planter; co-founding pastor, Restore Community Church, Kansas City, Missouri

"Many of us want to find divine moments in the daily grind, yet they seem inaccessible or only for certain types of people. *Believe Boldly* serves as a guide written by a humble learner for those who want to learn how to cultivate a deeper relationship with the Holy Spirit. With practical examples and stories of experiencing the power of God through prayer, *Believe Boldly* offers women hope that Jesus is able to change our hearts to live out His love in powerful ways."

Jessica Leep Fick, author, *Beautiful Feet: Unleashing Women to Everyday Witness*

"Erica's words are the reminder that every 'normal' mom needs—a fierce truth that our unchanging God is no less present and miraculous for us in the midst of diapering and making peanut butter sandwiches than He was for Moses on the mountain top, and that He holds us just as dear."

Jenny Rapson, editor, ForEveryMom.com

"If the church has a 'lost art,' it's prayer. Erica pulls back the drapes of what it means to pray—really pray—and invites us all into that divine adventure. This is not a theoretical, analytical or philosophical book *about* prayer. This book *is* prayer, and in it Erica gives a real-life playbook for the real-life Christ follower. Simple and magnificent, current and timeless. Bravo, Erica!"

Paige Henderson, co-founder,
Fellowship of the Sword Ministries

"Erica Willis truly is one of those people who oozes Jesus. As she shared her journey into complete obedience and abandonment to Holy Spirit, I realized I was asking myself, 'Sam, are you seeking Holy Spirit like that?' As you read, my prayer is that what Father has done in Erica will encourage you to fix your eyes on Him and jump into all that He invites you to."

Sam Perry, worship pastor and lover of the Bride;
founder, BackPorchMinistries.org

"Erica's excitement for God comes through in every line of *Believe Boldly*. She has experienced the power of prayer and surrender to the Holy Spirit in amazing ways, and she invites you, through this book, to embark on your own journey with God. With relatable stories and infectious joy, Erica shares from her heart and encourages us to take bold steps of faith and believe Him for more—of everything."

Rachel Anne Ridge, author, *Flash: The Homeless
Donkey Who Taught Me about Life, Faith, and
Second Chances* and *Made to Belong: A 6-Week
Journey to Discover Your Life's Purpose*

believe
BOLDLY

believe
BOLDLY

THE POWER OF
SIMPLE, CONFIDENT
PRAYER TO UNLEASH
THE SUPERNATURAL

ERICA WILLIS

Chosen

a division of Baker Publishing Group
Minneapolis, Minnesota

© 2018 by Erica N. Willis

Published by Chosen Books
11400 Hampshire Avenue South
Bloomington, Minnesota 55438
www.chosenbooks.com

Chosen Books is a division of
Baker Publishing Group, Grand Rapids, Michigan

Printed in the United States of America

Library of Congress Cataloging-in-Publication Data
Names: Willis, Erica, author.
Title: Believe boldly : the power of simple, confident prayer to unleash the supernatural / Erica Willis.
Description: Minneapolis, Minnesota : Chosen, 2018.
Identifiers: LCCN 2017038732 | ISBN 9780800798628 (trade paper : alk. paper)
Subjects: LCSH: Prayer—Christianity. | Faith.
Classification: LCC BV210.3 .W54 2018 | DDC 248.3/2—dc23
LC record available at https://lccn.loc.gov/2017038732

Cover design by Emily Weigel

18 19 20 21 22 23 24   7 6 5 4 3 2 1

To Joey, the man who captured my heart but
never tried to tame it.

Contents

CONTENTS

Part Three: A Spiritual Launching Pad

Foreword

Our world doesn't fully understand Christianity right now. Some look at faith and wonder if it is contained in a church building. Others decide that if it is what is portrayed on social media, they will pass. Others long for truth and hope, but it feels as though Christianity is for only those who have it all together.

But what about us, those who call ourselves believers?

Sometimes we can get just as tangled in what *looks* like Christianity.

That is why I love *Believe Boldly* so much. It is an honest look at how we linger right on the edge of what Jesus promised, when He is inviting us to jump into the deep with Him. It feels as though I am sitting with a good friend as we unwrap the amazing promises Jesus shared.

As I write these words, I have just returned from a weekend of ministry. Women flew and drove in from all over the nation. All weekend long we soaked in the beauty of the rustic, secluded ranch where we stayed. We explored the promises of God. We prayed.

These are women who long to make a difference in the world with their faith. They drove long distances because they want to follow Jesus, wherever He leads, whatever He asks, whatever miracle He wants to do in or through them. They understand that Jesus loves them and that He rescued them.

They dare to believe there is even more than that initial and beautiful encounter with Jesus.

Jesus invites His followers to encounter Him daily—with strangers, in our relationships, in our homes, in our workplaces and in the hardest parts of ministry. He invites us to listen for His voice and surrender in response.

He asks us to believe that His promises are for today.

We are called and compelled to be salt and light in a world that doesn't understand Him but is seeking truth.

That is why *Believe Boldly* resonates in my soul. It is a song that plays over me while I go about my daily routine, wearing my OU T-shirt and yoga pants, my hair in a ponytail. I am an ordinary woman who loves Jesus, yet I dare to believe that when we believe, we are loosed to live our faith boldly.

Our faith changes us, and then it changes the world around us.

If you are spiritually hungry for all that Jesus offers . . .

If you long to walk with other women who long to make a difference with their faith . . .

If you are crying out for God to restore the joy of your salvation . . .

Believe Boldly just might be the spark that begins that beautiful work in you and through you.

I believe that God is raising up an army of Jesus followers to live our faith shoulder to shoulder. Loving him. Loving the world tangibly. Believing boldly *together*.

Suzanne Eller, international speaker and blogger;
author, *Come with Me: Discovering the Beauty
of Following Where He Leads* and *Come with Me
Devotional: A Yearlong Adventure in Following Jesus*

Acknowledgments

First and foremost, I would like to thank my husband, Joey. No matter how big or crazy my ideas sound, you never bat an eye. Thank you for giving me space to write. There will be an extra jewel in your crown for every time you said, "Whatever you need, I've got your back."

To my kids, whose lives are such an intricate part of my faith story: You are my inspiration, and I cannot cuddle you enough to convey my deep love for you. I hope the hours invested in this book while you are little will be inspirational as you grow up knowing that following Jesus does not mean always getting to do the "fun thing."

I would like to thank Kim Bangs and the entire Chosen Books team for investing in bringing my voice to the Baker Publishing world. You have all supported my story and viewpoint from day one. I remember the day God told me I would be publishing my book with you. It is fantastic to see that come to fruition. A special thanks to my editor, Kathryn Deering, who filtered all my excitement and candor (!!!) into material that is both endearing and inspiring. I love how God used the strong voice in you to bring out the best in me.

This book would not have had a launching pad without my coaches, leaders and participants from #theFives. To my coaches: No one will ever know the hours you have sacrificed developing spreadsheets, praying over names and missing time with your loved ones to further the cause of prayer across the United States. Jesus saw every late-night text and heartfelt comment you shared. Way to run your race! To my leaders: Thank you for stepping up to lead even when you were scared or unsure of your abilities. You are bold and strong, and lives have been changed by your example! To those who participated in #theFives: Early-morning prayer has never been easy for me, but your encouraging comments and prayers have moved more than one mountain. Never give up, especially when that alarm goes off at 5:00 a.m. I am cheering you on!

Thank you to Restore Community Church for training and sending Joey and me into our next phase of ministry when we had no idea what that would be. The way you celebrate those you send is refreshing and inspirational. I pray more churches will catch the vision of the big "C" church as you have.

Thank you, New River Fellowship, for opening my eyes to a world I had yet to discover. Under your leadership I have been shaped and refined for the new gifts God had been waiting to release in me. Thank you for giving me a voice, a platform and a warm hug when I needed one.

I want to thank my family for their support: my dad, Mike, and my stepmom, Jill. My stepdad, Todd. My brother, Anthony. My in-laws, Jackie and Sheila, my sis-in-law, Mandy, and my brother-in-law, Jeremy. To every friend who watched my kids while I wrote, cooked dinners for my family, proofread my work and sent me encouraging texts when I wanted to quit: You have a special place in my heart.

Last but not least, thank you to my mom, Jaymee. I made it to Central Park.

PART ONE

MY DOUBTING HEART

one

Normals vs. Supers

"Anything, God. I will do it. Just show me what is next. There has to be more!"

Carpet fibers pressed into my face as my tears soaked my living room rug. I ached with a hunger for more of God, for answers and direction from Him. But all I heard was silence. Facedown with arms limp by my side, my posture embodied my lifeless faith.

I was drained, hopeless and grasping at straws.

I had fallen on my face that morning because I needed a change only God could bring. My faith and all it held was, well, boring. I wanted more, *needed* more. I was a stay-at-home mom who served as a church children's ministry director. My husband, Joey, was a full-time student, full-time banker and full-time church leader. The days were too short and my sleep at night even shorter. While I could see God working in my ministry and family, it was not enough. The God of the New Testament was not as present as I hoped He would be. With all my heart, I wished to see the miracles of the Bible in my little ministry and my suburban family.

My faith was average. I had become *normal*. Ugh. Normal is milquetoast Christianity. Someone *please* spit me out of my lukewarm existence.

Where were the miracles of the Bible?

Whom had I touched who was healed from sickness?

Why could I not identify real spiritual warfare?

My friends were being baptized into the faith, but I watched them continue to struggle to believe. They were strapped into a rollercoaster of continual highs and lows, driven by their circumstances. This did not look like the victorious life Christ promised us. There had to be more. People in the New Testament laid their hands on strangers and watched as their legs and eyes and hearts were restored. It was a daily occurrence. Where was that in my life? Had I strayed from His original design? Out of my need to keep my encounters with God predictable and manageable, had I suppressed the supernatural?

That morning I finally came to understand that my life had become a series of safe encounters with God—calculated, formulated, *under*whelming.

I could not stand it anymore. It had to change.

The Normals

I think of myself as a realist. I like facts and figures. I enjoy a good debate about theology. I am balanced and fair and have a good head on my shoulders. Long before I take a step, everything has been weighed, calculated and planned in my head. I am concise, logical and I get straight to the point.

The only problem for people like me is that God does not always speak to our brains first. Sometimes He bypasses our intellects and speaks straight to our hearts. Unfortunately, I can be *all* brain.

Maybe you are like that, too. Many people are. I lovingly call it being "a Normal." Things in your life make sense and you like it that way. A little sway in the boat is okay, but you certainly do not rock it. You show up for church on Sundays and the sermon speaks to you, most days. You are safe and predictable, exactly the way God intended, right? I completely understand. God made us Normals mature and wise for a reason, but we tend to box ourselves in.

In high school I began to let my responsible and careful approach turn into a fear that poisoned and paralyzed me. I had been a cheerleader for five years when I decided to step up my game and learn gymnastics. I would spend an hour and a half after school in cheerleading practice, flying through the air as my squad tossed me in the sky like a rag doll. Up and down, up and down—the stunts we built with an all-girl squad were impressive. Then one day a week my friend Amanda and I would rush from practice, grab a fast-food burger to fuel our growth-spurt-driven bodies, and run into gymnastics class moments before it began.

The coach would start with warm-ups and stretches, getting our muscles prepared for an hour of running back and forth. We did V-sits, splits, supermans—a collection of exercises meant to prepare and condition us. Every girl in the class lined up at one end of the floor and took turns running toward the coach. He was poised to catch each girl around the waist as she flipped in the air. I loved the round-off-into-back-handspring combination. Focused and determined, I ran with speed and correct alignment and usually pulled it off without a hitch.

However, I was terrified to tumble on anything but that bouncy, padded, royal blue floor. It made me feel safe and brave—unlike when I was actually cheering. The track encircling the football field where we did stunts every Friday night? A little bouncy, but nothing like the tumbling floor. The wooden basketball court that we performed on at halftime all spring? Please do not get me started on that death trap. I would rather break my own neck than let the floor do it for me!

That royal blue floor became my safety net and it eventually trapped me for good. As long as I was in my controlled environment with cushion and a spotter, I was good. Take me out of my comfort zone and I lost all sight of what I knew and understood to be true. I did not like to venture outside of those boundaries. I would step off the practice floor and stop thinking of myself as a gymnast. I would question my ability and forget all I had accomplished over the past several years. Convinced of my impending doom, I only did one back handspring at a game in my whole high school cheering career.

One.

Years of practice and thousands of dollars down the drain. At game time, all those hours of hard work, sweat and risk amounted to nothing. Not because I was incapable, but because I was scared of the risks. On the gymnastics floor with a paid professional, I was invincible. I was not scared to venture into a new skill or jump higher. My spotter had my back and I knew I would not fall. Those firm hands around my waist gave me the courage I needed to try daring stunts. But I could not attempt anything otherwise.

I felt I needed to protect my Normal self. I filtered every encounter—physical or spiritual—through my own Normal definition of myself, rather than looking to Christ for my identity. What about you? Can you identify with this approach to life? Is God calling you to take some spiritual risks? What is He asking you to try? Where is He leading you to step out of your comfort zone? His hands are securely on you. You will not break your neck!

Let's open our minds to the possibility that there is more out there. Let's stop letting our fears dictate our destiny.

The Supers

Normals like me do not normally know what to make of people who seem to love the super-spiritual stuff. I call them the Supers. Supers seem to come from a different planet. They feel the excitement of the Lord; in fact, they crave it. These are the people in your church or Bible study who use different terminology such as, "baptism in the Spirit" and "holy laughter." They may say things like, "I had a dream from God about you last night," and "God gave me a word for you."

A "word"? Interesting.

For someone like me who had never heard of such things, statements like this could be intimidating and overwhelming. I did not know whether to trust the Supers or dismiss them altogether. They pushed my Normal meter over the edge. I resorted to snarky thoughts rather than trying to understand what they were saying. Their view of the world was so different from my own. To them, everything seemed to have a purpose. Every butterfly that floated by told a story of God's love. Each spoken word had the power to heal or kill. Some claimed God even ordained what time of day they would go to the grocery store (*Really? You think God cares about the exact moment you walk down the produce aisle? Grab a head of lettuce and move on, lady!*)

I could not understand them. They were so intense! Did they ever just turn on the television and zone out for a bit? My brain would be on overload if I tried to make a lesson out of everything I touched or tasted. Each time someone would share a story of God speaking through some unexpected means, I would roll my eyes (on the inside) and look around the room for a friend to save me from the nonsensical conversation.

21

Then there are "spiritual dreams." We Normals see our dreams as out of our control and often weird. Why would we think a dream about pink elephants was a revelation from God? Was that a message from the Holy Spirit—or from the late-night pizza? To keep it safe, I filed "Dreams" under "Supers" and moved on.

Then there were those pretend languages that people claimed to have received directly from God. What? This had to be a joke. So-called prayer languages sounded like babble to me. All the super-spiritual stuff just felt a little crazy.

Until one day, it was not.

Taste and See

My husband, Joey, is stacked and lean. With muscles for days, he thrives in the gym and enjoys a good workout. As good as he looks, most people would be shocked to know he is addicted to sweets. Candy? He's down. Ice cream? Of course the average person eats half a gallon at one sitting, right? Joey once devoured an entire specialty ice cream treat created to feed ten people *all by himself.* When we have friends over for dinner, he is always in charge of our dessert. As far as I am concerned, this is a great arrangement in our marriage. For starters, I do not really care about dessert. Joey is very particular about the amount of time a fresh Toll House cookie sits in the oven. His cookies are the perfect balance of baked, but still gooey. I refuse to strive for his level of perfection. Ain't nobody got time for that.

When I was growing up, there was a strict limit on sweets in my home. My mom baked often, but we were never permitted to go crazy with the sugar intake. Two cookies a day, tops. And make sure you play in the yard for an hour to run it off. I had a built-in sugar regulator. Being the firstborn child, a Type A person, this pleased me.

Then I married Joey. In our first year of marriage, he would bake a cake at 10:00 p.m. just because it sounded good. Who bakes a cake that late? Who has energy enough to stay up late, make a mess of the kitchen, wait for it to bake, let it cool, eat it, and then clean up the mess? Certainly not me! Joey never counted the cost of sleep or cleaning. He would create his masterpiece with love and care, and the smell of goodness would fill our tiny apartment.

The first time this happened, I truly believed he was out of his mind. *Everything in moderation, you animal!* Cake must come directly after dinner, paired with a glass of milk. It does not fit as a midnight snack.

Then I tasted the warm cake, iced just out of the oven. . . . Oh. My.

My eyes were opened to a whole new world, and my waistband to a whole new size. How glorious! How magnificent! How . . . how . . . how could I get more? We decided from then on there was no need to cut "slices" of cake. That was for amateurs. Anyway, who wants only *one* piece of warm yellow cake? Just grab a knife and hack away whatever size chunk you want!

I never knew how delicious warm cake at midnight was until I tasted it for myself. In the end, it turned out that Joey was right: Late night cake is the best cake. But I could not have known just how good if I had never tasted it for myself.

It is like that with God, too: "Taste and see that the Lord is good. . . ." (Psalm 38:4).

The Holy Spirit has a big ol' cake waiting for you. Not day-old cake. Fresh cake, right out of the oven, made just for you. You may have your own method of how you indulge in God, and it may look nothing like the Supers. They sit for hours reading their Bible or randomly praying for people on the street. That does not look appetizing to you. Your anxiety may skyrocket when you think of the mess it could make. You have to ask yourself:

It is worth all that work to experience more of the Holy Spirit?

May I suggest a risky thought? If I open my responsible adult mind to the possibility that God is wilder than we understand, I will begin to see it with my own eyes. When they are not busy rolling into the back of my head at the absurdity of it all, I may have a chance to look into the face of God. There are no boundaries to our Holy Spirit encounters. It almost seems indulgent and irresponsible to open up to such things as visions and dreams, but it is not. If there is anything I have learned about late-night cake, it is this:

What we unleash through indulgence we will never manifest through calculated encounters.

Taste and see that He is good.

The Retreat

On my weather app the weekend forecast was filled with cloud icons and miniature lightning bolts. But this was not just any weekend. It was the three days for which I had been praying, planning and earnestly seeking direction for months. It was the first retreat I had ever created, and I wanted it to be perfect.

I would be leading eighty women in worship and prayer. Most of them had never met each other in person before; they were part of a nationwide prayer accountability ministry called #theFives that I had felt led by God to launch. I was excited for these women to meet for the first time. I wanted each one to have a fresh encounter with Him. They needed time to rest in His presence that weekend so they could hear His voice lovingly speaking to them.

But ugh, those tiny clouds! I had such grand plans. Our prayer times were supposed to be out in the Texas sunshine, reveling in the blooming bluebonnets, not indoors trapped in bunk beds. And what about the pool party? The good Lord knows every killer retreat has a pool party. . . .

Yet storm clouds were coming. Brilliant.

Why is it that when we expect God to show up in a certain way, He always exchanges our plans for His own? It does not make it easy to run the show. I had asked God to direct every piece of the retreat, and He had picked the weekend. He had picked the location. He had chosen the women who would attend. And yet, clouds.

That weekend forecast was right on. No blue sky peeked through the thick layer of rain clouds. All weekend. I felt despondent. Lack of control always makes me cranky. I could control many things, but the weather was not one of them. I had to decide: would I let this ruin my weekend? Would I let it consume my thoughts and take my focus? I had to remember that the weekend was about enabling women to bravely encounter a side of God they did not know existed. No rain was going to stop that.

I chose to be content with God's sovereignty. No matter if the retreat was inside or outside, He knew what He was doing. The whole first day went by without a drop; not even a misting. That evening we gathered together for worship as I taught on how God knows the most intimate details of who we are and loves us despite our shortcomings. He simply offers His hand as we walk this life together. I shared how we feel scared of God and easily forget that He is a loving Father who welcomes us.

I prayed for every woman in the room to join me, inviting them to come forward if they wanted to feel the love of God unrestrained by fear. As I prayed aloud, a soft "ting" sound began to ring from the rafters above. The tin roof of the building started singing.

It was raining.

It quickly grew into a roar. It was as if the heavens had opened up just for us, in this sacred moment. Although the dreaded rain had finally materialized, it was now a beautiful symbol of how the Holy Spirit, who is often represented by water, was cleansing these women from their past fears and moving them into newness of life.

As long as the women were still climbing down the steps to the lower platform where I stood, drops of water pelted the metal roof. It was like a joyful symphony between nature and God. The women wrapped their arms around one another as they prayed fervently for new and trusting faith. Time passed. Eventually, as soon as the floor was cleared and the women were back in their seats, the rain stopped.

Immediately.

It ended up being the only time we had rain all weekend long. Six months earlier I would not have noticed this moment as being anything more than coincidence. Now? We had just experienced a special moment; God had revealed Himself through the rain.

All of us knew that we had just experienced something supernatural. Far from being supernatural in a strange or weird way, it was wonderful. We sat in the silence that followed, refusing to interrupt a moment that felt sacred and holy. The presence of God was more tangible there than I had ever experienced, and deep down I knew it was only the beginning. God had given me a sneak peek of His vast power—power that would continue to grow in expression if I let down the walls I had built around my faith. I would not have to throw away the truths of His Word or dismiss wisdom altogether in order to view God from a perspective I had never considered before.

God is supernatural, after all. Who would want Him to be anything else? Not only can He reform the way we think and move and love, He can do it for eighty women at the same time, underlining His power with a pounding rainstorm. He loves us, and He brings heaven to earth.

When Jesus walked the city streets as a flesh-and-bone man, He did not keep the super-spiritual stuff for Himself. On the contrary, He opened heaven's floodgates and rained down miracles. He gave sight to the blind and grace to the condemned. He filled empty stomachs and empty hearts. This was beyond the people's experience or expectation, and no one could explain it—except to shake their heads in awe. God had joined them in their humanity to make Himself known to them. His presence among sinful humans would continue to prove that God is not predictable.

God Is Not a How-To Book

Like me, you too may be a Normal. Being a Normal is okay. Your faith is safe and comforting, bringing you much hope and revelation daily. Your salvation is secure and you can hear God when He speaks. These are all great, lovely things. But what if there is more revelation and power for you as you live out your faith? Yes, God is responsible and even predictable at times, but what if He wants to express His untamable wildness through His faithful followers—including you?

If you knew God wanted to perform miracles through your hands, would you be open to it? What if others will be led to faith in Jesus because of a supernatural movement of God through you? Would you choose to expand your current beliefs to include seemingly strange encounters for the sake of sharing the Gospel? Because try as we may, we cannot box God into our comfort zone. He sets the boundaries, not us.

Even if you are much like me in my Normal days, dutiful (and, truth be told, kind of dull), you may be starting to reconsider things. Maybe it is time to push the boundaries of "safe and predictable." Maybe it is time to stop ignoring the spiritual side of reality.

We are familiar and comfortable with the world we inhabit, but we know there is more. We may be timid about exploring, but we recognize the fact that our spiritual lives matter more than our physical lives. We should not be shocked if the supernatural feels unnatural, because we have become so thoroughly rooted in what we can see and touch and control. God does not come to fill our mold, but to shatter it.

I look back now on Normal Erica and I am sad. I missed out on so much. It was easy to label the things of God that made me uncomfortable as "crazy" instead of opening myself up to them and asking God what He was trying to show me. It was easy to describe supernatural things as "unbiblical." (Heck, I did it for years. That is how I had been taught.) My identity was wrapped up in being a Normal, grounded and trustworthy. It was as if I had written a pamphlet titled, "All You Ever Need to Know about God" and passed it out to everyone I knew.

Now I needed to burn every copy.

Our God is not a pamphlet or a how-to book. Neither is *Believe Boldly*. This book is a kick starter for your faith. It is a reminder that God will not be contained or mapped or controlled, only chased after. The only way we can find the fullness of life in Him is to push the limits, break out of our comfort zones and be open to whatever He might want to say or do. It may look sweaty and undignified, but who cares? He is our goal, the center of everything. And He invites us to engage with Him more deeply.

It is worth every struggle to find more of God. He will meet us more than halfway once we decide that we want to live a more supernatural life.

Are you ready for more?

Check Your Pulse

1. Do you have a powerful or powerless faith? In what area do you feel your faith is lacking? In what area is it strong?

2. Would you consider yourself a Normal or a Super? For what reasons?

3. If you could choose how God would move in a supernatural way in your life, what would you ask Him to do?

4. When was the last time God called you out of your comfort zone to follow Him?

5. Confess any preconceived judgments you have against either Normals or Supers, and ask God to give you a clean slate.

two

Do Not Be Afraid
of the Dark

I glanced at my calendar for space to squeeze in coffee with a friend.

This week was no good. Next week was jam-packed, too.

Scroll, scroll with my thumb leading my phone to the next month. Really? A whole month away? How could I not have a single hour to share with a friend in need of connection?

It was then I knew I had a problem. It is called "Fill-Every-Moment-of-Every-Day-Itis."

I do not like to sit at home and twiddle my thumbs. With a happy little girl by my side, we pack up and go every day. The zoo, the pool, the only indoor play area that does not smell like pee, wherever. We are regular world travelers. If Chick-Fil-A took passports, ours would be stamped to the max, marking our adventures with sticky fingers and chicken nugget meals. We live free and open, setting our own daily to-dos.

Yet here I was, too scheduled to schedule.

How was that even possible? Was I so social that I had no room to be more social? Something had to give. Shaving down the packed calendar was not going to be easy.

My people need me, Lord! These women I serve cannot do this alone. It is my job to take them under my wing and love them as You would love them. Meeting with a woman while sipping a cup of fantastic coffee can do more than people understand. I need to make space for them. You created me to pour myself into the lives of women, drinking endless handcrafted coffees along the way. How can I serve everyone You call me to? There are not enough hours in the day.

God quietly reminded me that I was not, in fact, God, and He would take care of any needs that clearing my schedule left open. Had I forgotten that He had other people who could serve the women of our church as well? I was not a one-woman show, after all. And when was the last time I made room in my calendar for a coffee hour with Him? Were my priorities aligned to follow Him, or was I following my own agenda?

Wrong priorities and subconscious pride. What a destructive combo.

I was swinging on a tricky trapeze, a ministry pendulum between seeking and serving. Seeking God is not the same as serving Him. Counseling in the the name of Jesus all day was beginning to make me believe that I had spent time with Jesus. This is not true. Just because I may talk about my husband all day does not mean I am with my husband all day. How easy it is to forget this obvious truth. I could not be the minister God called me to be without intimate time spent with Him. It is out of the overflow of our time together that I would serve the body of Christ. No prayer and quiet time = No effective ministry.

Because of my calendar craziness, spending time with Jesus frequently took a back seat to talking about Jesus. It was not my intention to make Him second, but it happened more than I liked. I was beginning to see that when my life spiraled out of control on my calendar, my heart lost hope in the hustle. The noisy world drowned out His voice, and it would be the death of my faith if I did not do something. I needed consistent time with God, as soon as possible. But how could I make time?

I woke each morning to the sound of my crying toddler daughter, Reese. The whirlwind compounded as Tristan, my five-year-old son, crankily entered the living room, refusing to accept that kindergarten was his full-time gig. Then it was time to pack his school lunch and kiss hubby Joey as he went out the door, moving on to school drop-off and pick-up, Play-Doh and playgrounds, wipe-up, lift-up, cook-up, till the moment when Joey would finally walk back through the door to share the burden of our busy home. The evenings were filled with church ministry or Joey studying. Late to bed, early to rise. I was a flurry of movement from morning till bedtime.

Where is my calendar going to open up, God? There isn't space anywhere. . . . Note to self: Be careful what you ask.

Before long, our pastor challenged Joey to get up early to pray for an hour before his busy day began. They would keep each other accountable by texting a wake-up message bright and early. It sounded like a noble goal to seek God in early-morning prayer as Jesus had done, but in reality . . . ? Joey already went to the gym at 5:30 a.m., which moved up his new alarm setting to 4:30 a.m.

Lord, help us.

Did our pastor realize what my husband's schedule was like? Late-night study sessions to sunrise prayer? This sounded like a ticking time bomb. Yet Joey was determined to try it.

"This is the stupidest thing you have ever done. Seriously. When will you sleep? How will you function? How are you going to help me with the kids when you are exhausted?" All the wifely empathy and support I had ever mustered quickly disappeared.

Supportive wife, party of one.

One week went by and he stuck with it. His resolve did not dissolve. He rose faithfully at 4:30 a.m. each day. In fact, he was in a better mood than when he slept longer. The way he spoke to us was different. His current schedule of school and work and church planting no longer overwhelmed him. He was a changed man, all from praying for an hour each morning before he hit the ground running. This prayer thing was shifting our home life.

Shocked wife, party of one.

Not one to be outdone, I thought long and hard about transforming my own habits. It was time for a change. Clearly, God was working a miracle here, and I did not want to miss out. I set my alarm to wake up before sunrise alongside my husband. The buddy system is key to our faith, especially when following Jesus into lifestyle changes.

This is madness, I declared to myself. *The fiction of following God is always prettier than the reality.*

That next morning, I shuffled downstairs and brewed strong coffee, hoping it would help keep me awake. I situated myself upright on the couch so I would not fall asleep. I prayed out loud and with my eyes wide open so I could not drift off. After praying for the basics of family, finances, faith, I was out of words. I snuck a sideways glance at the giant round clock on the wall.

Ten minutes.

Ten minutes? I had been praying for only ten minutes? Oh no—praying was harder than I had thought. Who else could I pray for? Maybe the president? I had never done that before. Do people pray for their pets? Maybe the weather? *Lord, save us from the mosquitoes this summer.*

Praise God that His works are not dependent upon our eloquence.

That first day was downright difficult. It did not feel holy or special. No angels appeared to applaud my efforts. The heavens did not open to reveal a descending dove. I was not glamorous or trendy, sitting on my stained couch in my yoga pants with bags under my eyes. Far from being a supernatural encounter with God, that hour consisted of plain, old-fashioned obedience, the nitty-gritty of faith. But it was a step in the right direction. If I wanted to create space in my calendar to hear from God, 5:00 a.m. was the only time slot available between "Passed-Out Exhausted" and "Crying Baby Alarm." This was clear. Now my job was to follow through.

The next morning I showed up for prayer with more to say. The morning after that, I had a teeny-tiny moment of revelation from God. Bit by bit, the pieces of a real relationship with God began to fall into place. Not only was I talking, but I was listening.

In my mind I began to hear the difference between my own voice and God's. Who knew I could know with certainty what God was saying, with no second-guessing? I could not get enough of my early morning time with God. An hour was no longer enough. I would find myself interrupted by my kids waking up at 6:30 a.m. and I was far from finished.

It was a miracle.

I craved that daily space, just me and God, no distractions. The more I pressed in, the more I could hear His whisper, not just in the morning, but all day long. When I needed guidance on what to say or how to say it, wisdom came quickly. I was feeling Him more, seeing His hand in all the little things. This was a radical faith, and it came through obedience and sacrifice, as modeled by Jesus.

Jesus Led the Way

The concept of early-morning prayer is not new. It does not carry the latest hipster hashtag—#yawningforYahweh. Jesus himself established the precedent of praying before anyone else awoke. In the early-morning prayer, He sought connection with his Father: "Very early in the morning, while it was still dark, Jesus got up, left the house and went off to a solitary place, where he prayed" (Mark 1:35).

Jesus was not afraid of the dark. In fact, as we see in the Bible, He sought it out. Time after time, Jesus arose before dawn to seek His Father. Without the aid of an iPhone alarm, His yearning was enough to wake Him up from His sleep while it was still dark. He needed to talk with His Father—no ifs, ands or snooze button(s).

A radical prayer life does not appear magically. Even Jesus' prayer times did not happen accidentally. Besides solitude, His times of prayer required forethought and self-discipline. The verse does not explain how long He prayed or what words He said, probably because that is not the point anyway. God wanted to show us the heart of Jesus, from which everything flows, that kept seeking after the Father no matter the inconvenience or time of day.

When your need to hear from God overshadows your need to sleep, you have everything you really need. That guidance you long for? Found. The peace that calms you in the face of trials? Granted. Much-needed wisdom? Given in abundance.

Jesus shows us how to pray: "But Jesus often withdrew to lonely places and prayed" (Luke 5:16).

Jesus' priority for prayer reflected His position. He knew His purpose in coming to earth was that of an offering, a blameless sacrifice on the cross for our sins. Jesus understood that being perfect, in thought and deed, was no small responsibility. He was not about to risk our salvation on His potential slip-ups. Jesus knew He could do nothing good apart from God. Time connecting with His Father gave Jesus wisdom under the weight of the world. Prayer was a nonnegotiable.

What about you? What responsibilities do you carry that require wisdom from God? Maybe you are the CEO of a company, making decisions that affect a large number of lives. Are you raising small children, shaping their tiny hearts with every word you say (or do not say)? What about simply managing your own thoughts and reactions? Does that not warrant a passionate pursuit of daily prayer? For me, that daily time came at 5:00 a.m. For you it may be right before bed. The key ingredient to successful prayer is that it must be distraction-free. When the world is still sleeping, you can hear God's voice guiding you into all you need to know.

Seek the lonely places.

Jesus did.

So should we.

Although it can seem like a daunting prospect, we do not need to be afraid of the dark. We need not worry about failing or fumbling for the right words. God wants us to succeed, and He will help. He whispers, "Come away with me. Let down your guard. Do not be afraid to fail or fall. I am here. I bring light to the darkness. I never leave you or forsake you. Draw near to Me and I will draw near to you."

Jesus came to redeem the dark. My dark. Your dark. He shines a light into the hopeless and hurt parts of us—if only we will meet Him there. It takes self-discipline and prioritization to make that kind of relationship a reality, but it is worth every yawn and every cup of coffee. Transformation? Redemption? Satisfaction? All from a simple dedication to prayer?

Now that is a wake-up call I can get behind.

Let It Rain

All this early-morning prayer messed with my world. God started to talk to me about my habits, my family, my future.

More often than not, what I heard about myself stung. It was not comfortable. I knew that self-reflection is necessary if we are ever to grow, and without it we are condemned to live within our own selfish world view. God was transforming Joey and me and our family life.

Joey and I had committed to pray about the future during the five o'clock hour just as our life was at a crossroads: He would graduate from college in May, we were coming up on two years working at our church plant, our lease was up in six months and we were eager to know what our next steps would be.

During our individual prayer times, each of us felt that God was pointing to the month of August. So we needed to be on the lookout for change in August. Easy enough, right? Wrong. Waiting for August required more faith than we anticipated.

Change can be scary, but we did not want to let that deter us. We chose to take our unknown future as an invitation to pursue God more sacrificially. Our prayers shifted from "when" to "what" as we both begged for the same thing: more time to serve others in a ministry capacity. We could not make it all happen on our own.

We want to serve You more, God. We don't care about being rich. We want more time to follow the path You have laid in front of us. We will plant churches, serve the homeless, write, preach . . . whatever You ask. But we can't keep up with our current schedule. Everything gets only part of us; nothing gets our best.

We saw people in the Bible who prayed for rain to nourish their crops. The rain would grow their food supply larger so that they could feed not only their own families, but also others who did not have enough to eat. Joey and I were praying for "rain." We found a biblical precedent:

The prayer of a righteous person is powerful and effective. Elijah was a human being, even as we are. He prayed earnestly that it would not rain, and it did not rain on the land for three and a half years. Again he prayed, and the heavens gave rain, and the earth produced its crops.

James 5:16–18

"Make it rain on us," we prayed. "Shower us with time so we can invest in our own family as well as others. Let it rain, God!"

At first it felt strange to ask God to bless us—too bold, not humble enough. It did not matter that our motives were pure; the enemy was trying to twist the truth about our motives. Who are we not to ask for all that we can? God is our loving Father, and He graciously gives us good things when we ask according to His will. With our hearts in the right place, we can approach Him with confidence.

Halfway through August, we had almost given up trusting God. Out of the blue, Joey received a job offer without sending one resume. Not one. The biggest perk? His office hours were fewer than any job he had ever worked, yet we would still make enough salary for me to stay home with our children. I jokingly said it was a "fake job" because of the amount of free time it would allow him for ministry, while still receiving a full paycheck. God had given us exactly what we had prayed for.

He provided us with all we needed to continue serving Him, and more. We were reeling from His goodness to us, though we should not have been surprised. The Bible outlines God's loving character in Acts 14:17: "He has shown kindness by giving you rain from heaven and crops in their seasons; he provides you with plenty of food and fills your hearts with joy."

God's goodness is never-changing; His love is stable and reliable. But remembering that can be difficult. Yes, He had come through with the ideal job and I was beyond grateful, but I was not prepared for its location. God's blessing would be found only by moving to Texas, three states away from everything I held dear.

It was obvious that this was God's plan, but it certainly was not part of mine. I would never choose to live in Texas. Trusting God with this part of my future required deeper trust than ever. When we pray for blessing, we do not complain that it rained on our health but not our finances. We receive whatever God brings our way. I knew better than to tell the rain to pour here, where I already lived, and not there, in Texas. I had to follow God where He was leading, and there seemed to be a flashing neon sign illuminating a yellow-brick road away from my home sweet home in Kansas. I had to choose: obedience—or obstinance.

Joey and I decided to meet for lunch and discuss what should happen next. Was this truly God's next step for us? As I grabbed my keys and scooted into the driver's seat of my car, I offered up a prayer: *God, is this really You? Should we follow this job, or is it too good to be true? Do you truly want us to leave everything behind?*

Then I said a prayer I had never prayed before:

God, worship music has always guided me to Your will. Please confirm what You want us to do by speaking to me through the first song that plays on the radio.

To this day I do not know why I prayed those words. It was so out of character for me, and it seems a bit like looking into a crystal ball to see my future. I opened my Pandora app and pressed Play without looking at the next song. Loud and clear the refrain of the first song rang in my ears: "Let It Rain," by Jesus Culture.

It. Was. Perfect. God was confirming that the very rain we had prayed for over the past several months was indeed beginning to pour on us through the job offer. I surrendered it all right then and there. No negotiating. No holding back. *Risk it all!* I shouted inwardly, resisting the urge to run screaming for safety. This was going to be the greatest adventure of my life.

I was all in.

We said yes to the job, packed up everything we owned, and left behind my family, our friends and an established ministry we had helped build from the ground up—all in exchange for the unknown. No friends would be waiting to greet us on our front porch. We would not even have a front porch, since we lacked our own home as well. We were not headed to our next church, and I had no calling of my own that I would be fulfilling. We were not following some grand and well-explained plan. We were just being obedient to the next step.

More like cliff-diving to the next step.

The hardest steps require the most and explain the least.

#TheFives

Once in Texas, we kept our early-morning prayer time, but without the accountability of our church family who had prayed with us previously. It was terribly difficult, but we did it.

With the space of Joey's new work hours, I had time to follow through with a new endeavor: writing a blog. There was a tug in my heart to share with others my experience of early-morning prayer. When my pastor and I had shared our passion for prayer at our annual staff retreat back in Kansas City, the entire staff had latched onto the idea; they had implemented it among themselves and the entire church for a season. Who was to say there were not others out there who needed to know the power of consistent, sacrificial prayer?

I blogged all about the staff prayer group we had created in Kansas City, lovingly named "5 by 5 by 5." The goal was to wake at 5:00 a.m., text a little "Good morning!" to each other, and pray for an hour. The length of the commitment morphed into five days a week for five weeks, so that it would not be a prayer group with no beginning or end. This made it more accessible for the people of our church and left weekends as rest days.

Since my blog was still fairly new, I did not expect much of a response to my post. Yet in the Bible we see Jesus multiplying two loaves of bread and some fish into enough food to feed multitudes. He did the same with the meager beginnings of my prayer group. It eventually grew to hundreds.

We started small. One of my new Texas friends, Reneé, read my story. She shared that she was desperate for more prayer in her life, but with four kids she had difficulty making time for it each day. She asked if she could join me in praying early. We could keep each other accountable through a group text message as I had done in Kansas City. I was desperate for accountability, and adding someone new sounded fun.

I knew of a few other women who had participated in a five-week stint at our church in Kansas City who might want to join us. There we were, a small but mighty group of nine women, dedicated to our 5:00 a.m. wake-up call. It was the start of what we would eventually rename #theFives.

The first group was intimate and close to my heart, technology uniting my praying friends from my old stomping grounds in Kansas City with my new friends in Texas. Then the word spread about what God was doing through our early-morning prayers, and after that first five-week session, we began to grow. The next five weeks we were twenty-five people strong. Then forty-eight.

I did not feel qualified to lead it or manage that many voices, that many needs. I was in over my head and totally humbled. God began to give me wisdom about how to lead, and I watched as #theFives continued to spread to new states. It grew too large for one group text and too big for one leader. It was time to multiply.

Those of us who were in the first group stepped up to be leaders of our own accountability groups. We grew more. Seventy-two participants. A hundred and fifty participants. We invited more people to pray with us. #theFives stretched and grew and improved. The husbands of women in our groups begged for a men's group, so we added one. Our latest prayer session had over six hundred women and men praying at 5:00 a.m. in all U.S. time zones and in five countries.

#theFives changed everything. I mean everything. My family, my ability to hear God, what ministry looked like—it was broken down and rebuilt by God's hand. All because of an early wake-up call. I am not the only one. Hundreds of women and men have seen what simple, confident prayer can accomplish.

Obedience may be contagious, but it does not come easy.

I found that God can sustain you in all things, even where sleep is concerned. My entire life had to revolve around a 5:00 a.m. wake-up call, and at first I was not exactly excited about that sacrifice. It meant adjusting every part of my life to make room for that hour of prayer. The biggest struggle was getting past the lies I told myself: *I will never get up that early. . . . I am the worst morning person. . . . It will wake up my family. . . . I will get too tired. . . . I am too busy.*

God raised Jesus from the dead—surely, He can give me the energy I need for the day ahead. He is trustworthy when He says He will provide all that we need. He would not let me lose my mind from lack of sleep, and He will not let you lose yours. After all, God does His best transformations in the dark.

Redeeming the Dark

We have all heard this part of the Easter story: "Early on the first day of the week, while it was still dark, Mary Magdalene went to the tomb and saw that the stone had been removed from the entrance" (John 20:1).

That stone had been rolled away. He was risen from the dead. But have you ever noticed the time of day? God chose to reveal the resurrection of His Son earlier than the sunrise. That time of day carries deep significance. It is no coincidence that it happened in the early morning dark, just the time of day I saw God move miraculously to resurrect my faith through prayer. That pre-dawn hour is uniquely placed within our 24-hour day, and it shakes us awake. That is what those of us in #theFives have discovered, along with the early saints. It all goes back to Jesus' rising from the dead, which resulted in a revolution in the lives of His followers, a mighty movement of passion and truth.

You see, God did not stop raising the dead after He raised Jesus over 2,000 years ago. He resurrects *us* today. He resurrects us in the midst of our circumstances and struggles, our fears and failures. Just when you think the world has beaten you and stripped you of your true identity and left you for dead, God sweeps in and brings you back to life. He loves you more than you can imagine, bringing about your new life. But He does offer it. His love transforms you in a way that nothing else can. Breakthrough comes for you in the dark, just as it did with Jesus. No shadow can destroy you; no lack of light can keep Him away. The morning will reveal all the newness that has been reborn in the dark of night.

What about you? What darkness do you need freedom from? Where do you need direction? What is holding you back from consistent prayer?

I propose that you take an honest look at yourself and ask a tough question: *Am I willing to get up as early as needed to hear from God?*

Do you want an hour of extra sleep to be what holds you back from your resurrection? Following God means denying ourselves in order to do whatever He asks. I can confidently say it was worth every pain and sacrifice to encounter the supernatural movement of God. He uses me in unique ways now. Being a conduit to heal others, to receive prophetic dreams and visions, to speak in a prayer language that moves mountains—that is worth every 5:00 a.m. awakening.

I am here to tell you that when you surrender your right to your time and comfort so that you can chase after God, there is nothing that cannot happen for you or through you.

You do not need to be afraid of the dark. The God who loves you is waiting for you there.

Check Your Pulse

1. When do you normally pray? Do you hear from God during your prayer time?
2. What have you sacrificed, in the past or currently, for God?
3. What area of your life do you want God to transform?
4. Do praying and reading your Bible affect the way you live?
5. Pray and ask God what He wants you to sacrifice to make time for Him.

three

Baby Steps

My plastic Jelly sandals stuck to the hot pavement. The sidewalk of my elementary school was not very long, but to a kindergartener the hike to Mom's car seemed to take an eternity.

It was the last day of school. I could see Mom's face smiling from behind the oversized steering wheel as she waited in the pick-up lane. That smile was telling. I always knew when she had something up her sleeve. I popped open the sun-baked door of our white 1964 Cadillac De Ville, which creaked loudly as I pulled it shut.

Mom cheerfully announced, "We are headed to the lake! Change into your swimsuit."

Ah, the lake . . .

Summertime! Freedom! Those two words, "the lake," captured all of my excitement. And there in her hand was a fresh cherry limeade, ready to accompany me onto the sandy shore of the lake. Who could ask for more? I launched myself into the front seat, racing my brother for my favorite spot—that elevated space between the driver and passenger seat that we had lovingly named The Bump.

Nothing announced the goodness of summer like the hum of our car tires rolling through town, windows down, breeze in my hair. I made the quick change into my swimsuit on the floorboard of that Caddy, my tiny hands struggling to untangle the straps of my belly-baring bikini (hot pink fringe, anyone?). As we closed in on our destination, anticipation grew. Our arms were flung out windows like flying birds dipping and soaring in the wind. The doors opened. Tucking my Garfield beach towel under my arm, I raced to the water.

My toes hit sand, then pebbles, then water—then wave. Water equaled freedom. I was free!

That lake symbolized a new season. Having spent the school year indoors, regimented and structured—math, reading, recess, lunch—it was time for the Next. The Fresh. The Free. This was my "marker moment," and it was ushering in something new for me.

Those were the good old days of summer. It was a time in America when "a little color" was good for your children, so why not *slather* them in baby oil? Hurray for sunburns, inflatable rafts, secondhand smoke, and golden tans on all the Coppertone babies roasting near their sandcastles. The lake was good to us and we played there for hours.

On every lake trip, my mom brought a plastic spray bottle and kept it close. Before she laid out her towel or cranked up the volume on her boom box, she filled that spray bottle with chilled water from the lake. Whenever she felt overwhelmed by the heat, a few spritzes up and down her body made her good to go for at least another thirty minutes. (She was aiming for tan level "jerky.") After she decided that she had spent enough time in the blazing sun, she would slowly walk her body into the water—to her ankles, knees, waist, even her shoulders—but never over her head. Never so deep that the water might smudge her black, winged eyeliner.

The water from the lake gave all of us a reprieve from the scorching summer temps. Without it, we could not have spent as much time as we did under the Kansas sun.

Holy Spirit and Water

Like a cooling rush of water on hot skin, the Holy Spirit is just what we need to survive the heat of our faith journey. The Holy Spirit and water are closely linked. The Bible reminds us often of the connection. We are baptized by both, the Holy Spirit is described as Living Water, and we thirst for Him as a deer pants for a stream.

Several chapters in the book of Ezekiel tell a story about water flowing from a temple. In sort of a video-vision, God had taken the prophet Ezekiel to a place he had never been, and there he saw a man who gave him a detailed description of the temple.

Every word was recorded by Ezekiel as it was announced by the man, and, in true Old Testament style, everything was described in painstaking detail. We read lists of specific measurements, explanations of the order of events that are to take place inside the temple, and much about the priest's duties. (Think of it as *How to Build a Temple for Dummies.*)

At this point in this vision, the man revealing the details of the temple draws Ezekiel's attention to a river of water flowing from under the threshold of the temple. He leads Ezekiel to the river to measure the depth, but in order to get an accurate reading he has to get a little wet by standing right in the rushing water. Ezekiel tells us the story from his perspective:

As the man went eastward with a measuring line in his hand, he measured off a thousand cubits and then led me through water

49

that was ankle-deep. He measured off another thousand cubits and led me through water that was knee-deep. He measured off another thousand cubits and let me through water that was up to the waist. He measured off another thousand, but now it was a river that I could not cross, because the water had risen and was deep enough to swim in—a river that no one could cross. He asked me, "Son of man, do you see this?"

Ezekiel 47:3–6

Wow. Ezekiel was feeling like a human measuring tool at this point. But depth readings and building plans were not the only reason for this vision. The reason Ezekiel was not allowed to sit on the banks of the river? The man wanted Ezekiel to *experience* the water as he measured deeper and deeper, to feel the cool rush of fluid surrounding his ankles and flowing between his toes. As he stepped farther into the river, Ezekiel would have walked with more determined steps to keep his pace against the current, moving from his ankles . . . to his knees . . . up to his waist. . . . All along the way, the man measured and measured, guiding Ezekiel farther and farther. Finally, Ezekiel said, "No more." He could sense the pressure of the moving water, and he was afraid it would drown him.

The Spirit River

This river of water is a powerful illustration of the Holy Spirit. Flowing from the heart of the temple of God, the Holy Spirit is equal parts strength and refreshment. As Christians, we can look at this vision and begin to connect the dots in our own walk with God.

As Christians, our encounters with the Holy Spirit will feel much like Ezekiel's story. As God asks us to go deeper in our relationship with Him, we do want more, but we do not know where to start. Yet He gives us step-by-step guidance. All it takes are baby steps in the right direction. God does not require much—just a mustard-seed-sized amount of faith—in order to move mountains. The Holy Spirit is a gentleman. He will never force us to enter into something we do not desire. We can take baby steps into experiencing movement of the supernatural, at a pace we set ourselves.

What does this surrender to the Holy Spirit look like? Much like Ezekiel in the river. Initially, you tiptoe over to the anointing of the Holy Spirit, which seems like a rushing river of water, and you test the temperature and depth with a toe.

Not bad, you think to yourself. *I could get used to this.*

Next, feeling His movement through you, you step in with both feet. You begin to hear the Holy Spirit's voice with more clarity and can now sense Him giving you more direction. Surprisingly, you find that it does not feel at all scary or out of control. (If you are a Normal, you may have worried that an encounter with the Holy Spirit would make you like a maniac on a Holy Spirit mind trip, but this is not like that at all.) Your faith is growing deeper, and it is incredible to have the close support of your own personal Counselor.

You decide to go deeper. You wade in up to your knees. Not only does it feel refreshing, you now notice that the water is teeming with life. And you had never noticed those pretty little rocks hiding in the sand—suddenly they are one of the most beautiful creations you have ever seen. *How could I have missed them all these years?* The warmer waters of the shallows are comforting, while the cooler depths refresh you thoroughly. *But this isn't enough!* you cry out inside. *I want more!*

The Holy Spirit is calling you out still deeper. As the water swirls around your legs, you are gaining more insight into God's will for your life, and you are receiving more freedom from your past heart hurts. It feels exciting. You are braver, more empowered, less insecure about your place in the world. By now you are calling your friends to get into the water with you.

One foot in front of the other. Step after step. You choose to go deeper. *If it is this good in the shallow end, why wouldn't I want more?*

You travel farther and hit waist-deep water, which makes you suck in your abdomen. (Why is waist-deep water always the hardest?) Half of your body is now enveloped in the water. You are past the point of testing the waters and are now committing to swim. The saturation of the Holy Spirit begins to affect your sleep as you awake at odd hours to pray. He gives you visions and words to share, bringing life and hope to others. With the Holy Spirit in your heart, you no longer want to live in the world as you used to. You have learned that all you have to do is get yourself into the water in the first place. Once you are in, He will keep you afloat.

A Holy Current

As the Holy Spirit pours into every part of you, He asks for permission to do the thing He does best: Move you. This water is powerful and rushing, not to be taken lightly. Ezekiel could see it. He could feel it. Only the bravest of the brave step into the stream. It calls us out of our comfortable places. You no longer get to call the shots—His current guides you. On your part, it requires trust and release and a willingness to be vulnerable.

Oftentimes it takes a tragedy or dramatic shift in circumstances to make us willing to let go. Your kids are out of control. Your finances have tanked. Your marriage is falling apart. The difficulties of life are beating you down like the scorching sun, and you cannot find relief. No way can you mend and tie together all of the loose ends on your own, because you simply were not created to bear the burdens of life on your own.

Running out of options, you hear the soundless call: *Get in the water. Just one foot, if that's all you can manage. Then take another step.*

One foot in front of the other. Step after step.

When you get in up to your knees, you get beyond your fear. Now Wisdom steps in with you, and you begin to make wise decisions that help you fight the good fight, even when you feel you may drown.

Ah, now the water is up to your chest. God is present and you are thriving. He sustains you. God's Holy Spirit becomes your Counselor and Friend on a brand-new level. With Him, you can stay under that hot sun all day long if you need to. You lift your eyes to the swirling current ahead, and you understand that you can choose to turn back or keep going.

The man speaking to Ezekiel could have chosen to describe the depth of the water in words, but he did not. He wanted Ezekiel to feel it, to experience the water for himself, the shift and pull of the current and how it affected his balance. It is the same with us; we must experience the Spirit with our bodies if we ever hope to go deeper in our faith.

And it all starts with tentative baby steps.

The Water of Life

Our buddy Ezekiel went on to describe more about this river that brings life, though his mind could not comprehend it:

> Then he led me back to the bank of the river. When I arrived there, I saw a great number of trees on each side of the river. He said to me, "This water flows toward the eastern region and goes down into the Arabah, where it enters the Dead Sea. When it empties into the sea, the salty water there becomes fresh. Swarms of living creatures will live wherever the river flows. There will be

large numbers of fish, because this water flows there and makes the salt water fresh; so where the river flows everything will live."

Ezekiel 47:6–9

Here the man, seeing that Ezekiel was refusing to go farther into the depths of the river, walked him to the stability of the riverbank. He showed him the transition place far ahead where the river met the Dead Sea. Nothing could live in the Dead Sea because of the level of salt in the water. The seawater was desolate and stagnant. But look what happened when the living river transitioned into the Dead Sea: The river became clean and powerful and refreshing; all the salty water becomes fresh.

The river of life revives the sea of death. ("Where the river flows everything will live.")

When Ezekiel refused to budge deeper into the river, the man needed to inform and remind him of the reason the river exists in the first place: to bring life to the dead.

It is the same with us when the Holy Spirit resurrects our lifeless existence and infuses us with passion and purpose. Our hearts are brought back to life. Therefore, when it is our time to go deeper, we must overcome our fear of the unknown and understand the purposes of God. He wants us to experience more of Him. We must open our eyes to see the entire vision of how our obedience can help to change the lives of others as they watch us live out our testimony.

Your story is bigger than just you, and your life matters more than you realize.

Take Your Temperature

How far along are you in the river? How are you flowing with the Spirit?

When we enter into His living water and we are transformed, it will affect those around us. Our freshness becomes contagious. We bring it with us when we enter our workplaces, our homes, our kids' schools. Living out the abundant life found in the Holy Spirit will bring life to those around us. Those who are dead will find life.

Notice again what it says: "When it empties into the Dead Sea, the salty water there will become fresh." *When*, not *if*. If you are a believer, you must enter the water at some point.

The depth to which you are willing to walk in the river determines the amount of life you care to experience. If you drag your feet in the shallows, afraid of the current, then you will never live in true freedom. If you keep testing the water, afraid that the conditions are not what you want them to be, your cautious approach will curtail your progress.

For my part, I want to live, really *live*. I want to get a running start and *jump* into the river. Even if it seems a little scary at times, I want to experience life fully and abundantly. If I hold back, I will never find out who I was created to be.

"So where the river flows everything will live" (Ezekiel 47:9). What if you let go of your hesitation and jump into the deep water with complete abandon? What if you let the current of His Spirit carry you to the ocean, where His love is too vast to measure? How much life will He surround you with and how much life will He pour through you, all because you finally dove in?

A Skeptic's Swim Lesson

I used to be kind of a toes-only-in-the-water girl who did not know there was more. The Holy Spirit and I were buds, and I heard from Him on a regular basis. I would ask Him a question, He would answer and I would follow through in obedience.

Unfortunately, in my particular circle of friends that meant that I was deemed the super-spiritual one.

Holy guacamole! If I was the queen of the spiritual city, we were all doomed.

Because of this super-spiritual status, I never knew anything was missing. I thought I had the relationship with Holy Spirit that I was supposed to have as a "good Christian girl." I was just spiritual enough to never grow another day in my life. That is a terrifying place to be.

Until one day I asked the *wrong* question, which was exactly the *right* question: *God, I want more of you. What do you want from me?*

Dangerous questions decree powerful transformations. I was ready. I wanted more of Him. I was hungry for something new. I craved clarit,y and I was ready to do something radical.

God replied, *Are you willing to follow me wherever I lead, even if it looks nothing like what you expect?*

I laid it all on the line and said He could have it. *You can have all of me. All my dreams, my time, my plans.* My desire for God eclipsed the comfort I longed for. Although I had only my toes in the water, I felt as though I had plunged neck-deep in His river and its current was sweeping me away.

You see, until that moment, I had always been a skeptic when it came to hearing God through others.

I knew I could trust my own heart and mind because of the clarity with which I received revelation from Holy Spirit. When God spoke to me, I knew what it felt like and sounded like. My mind was sane, my motives pure, my relationship with God solid and trustworthy. I had written SAFE on my own forehead.

But you, random person on the street, I could not trust. How could you possibly hear from the Holy Spirit? What if you were crazy or on drugs?

You, friend, were nice and all, but who knows if you truly heard the Lord as well as I did?

Excuse after excuse. Mistrust after mistrust. I had built a wall of pride around my heart that allowed in only the tiniest light of revelation using only the very specific method that I had mapped out for myself: (1) I will pray and ask God a question. (2) He will answer my question. (3) I will do what He says. (4) The end.

It was safe and foolproof and absolutely paralyzing.

It took no extra faith whatsoever to hear from God the way I had always heard from Him. My heart was never on the line. Yes, He might ask me to sacrifice something dear to me, but I had done that before and survived. But no curve balls, please. Keep it Normal.

Then suddenly I was no longer the one asking the questions. God was: *What if I speak to you through someone else? What if I ask you to trust My work in another person?*

Nope, God. I folded my arms together. *That's a no-go. I don't need some crazy person telling me what You said. I trust my method just fine.*

His reply: *But what if I want to break through your method? What if I want to show up for you in a new way? Would you hear Me?*

God and I had these conversations often after I surrendered everything. He knows my stubborn heart better than anyone else. He also knows it is equally obedient—eventually. After some waiting, I always come around.

One day, before I had changed my answers to His questions, He sent His messenger to me in the form of a beautiful blond woman with a joy that could not be denied. Her name was Halli. She was one of "those" people whose faith made me nervous. She was nice, but I fully expected her to bring out the snakes at any moment; she was a little too "out there" for my sensible faith. Of course He would send someone like her.

I had set that morning aside to seek new revelation from God. He had been calling me to do this ridiculous thing that I had never done—write a book—and I was not about to be obedient without a fight. I was unqualified. Unprepared. Unsure. I had friends who were college English professors, and I could barely use a comma correctly. Surely He meant to ask *them* to write. Sure, I was a worship leader and a children's pastor and I loved to speak. But put the words down on paper and have the audacity to claim I was a writer? No way.

The Lord and I wrestled. I fought, kicked and screamed and cried an abundance of tears. Until I finally gave in that morning and said out loud, "Yes, God. I will write. Even though I don't understand and I am overwhelmed by my weakness, I will trust that You will come through for me."

That was that. Simple obedience through gritted teeth and tears.

As I came back from my time with God, still feeling the sting of my own shortcomings, I was swept up into the arms of the blond girl I barely knew. Halli said, "God gave me a word for you."

Oh, great. Someone with "an important message from the Lord." Here we go. . . .

"God told me you have a story to tell. He said to stop worrying about how it is going to happen, and know that it doesn't have to be perfect. Just tell your story."

I could not breathe.

What. Just. Happened?

Had God just spoken to someone else about my private moments with Him? How could anyone else possibly know about that?

Had I just heard a word from the Holy Spirit through a complete stranger?

This changed *everything*.

My walls came crashing down, along with my comfortable method of hearing from God. This girl's obedience to share what she had heard from the Lord had shattered my pride and showed me how calloused my heart had truly become. I was a completely broken and sobbing mess, runny nose and smeared mascara for the win. Did I mention I was also *not* a woman who cried easily? All the feels, people.

God had just proved that He did speak to other people, not only to me. He had just showed me that when others live out their faith in a radical way, it truly does bring life to the dead. He had just demonstrated to me the power of a fearless testimony.

This moment initiated my ankle-deep movement toward God in ways I could never have explained or put into a pretty, color-coded outline. God had messed up my plans and methods. He had begun to show me how beautiful He is in His unpredictability. I surrendered my will once again, and He welcomed me deeper into the river of His Spirit. I have never turned back.

What about You?

Are you afraid to know the depth of what the Holy Spirit can do for you and in you? Here are some truths you can stand on:

1. We know that God speaks to His people.

God does speak to us. As the 1984 New International Version puts it: "He who belongs to God hears what God says" (John 8:47). He speaks to anyone who is a Christian. The question is not if He is speaking, but whether or not we are we listening.

2. We are called to be obedient.

Jesus said, "Anyone who loves me will obey my teaching. My Father will love them, and we will come to them and make our home with them" (John 14:23).

Do you follow God? Is He the Lord of your life? Do you let Him run the show? Obedience is a nonnegotiable. When He speaks, we act in accordance.

3. God is not easily explained.

God has plans for us that cannot be fathomed. Therefore we cannot assume we have a handle on all the ways He wants to communicate with us. Paul reminds us that no eye has seen, no ear has heard and no human mind has conceived the things that God has prepared for those who love Him, that these things have been revealed to us by His Spirit (see 1 Corinthians 2:9). Are you ready to receive His revelation in whatever form He deems appropriate?

The River of Life is deep and wide—and uncontainable. His ways are higher than our ways. It may not make sense to our logical brains, but our hearts respond in a way that confirms His word. My moment of jumping into the river came in the form of a woman I barely knew. Yours may come to you in a sunset or a doctor visit. Whatever shape His word takes, listen to it. The Holy Spirit leads us into all truth, and He will reveal all you need to know.

Come, walk deeper. Come and sink deep into His love. Let the water rush overhead and bring life to all who gather around you.

Check Your Pulse

1. Think back on some of your favorite memories of water. It can be bath times, swimming in the pool, or lying on the beach. What did you love about it?

2. How can God be compared to water?

3. Describe your prayer time with God. Do you journal your prayers? Pray aloud, or silently? Listen to music, or sit in silence? How does God speak to you through your method?

4. Has anyone given you a "word from God" before? How did you react?

5. How would you describe yourself as a Christian: toes-in-the-water, completely underwater or somewhere in between?

four

Passion and Perseverance

My brother, Anthony, is the other pea in my pod. We are only thirteen months apart in age, so having him around was like growing up with a twin brother. I loved everything about him and still do. I wanted to wear the same clothes, do the same activities, and be best friends forever. We have story after story of the sort only siblings can share: embarrassing or deeply sad moments that no one else understands. Our bond is thick and strong, whether we talked last Sunday or last year. Nothing can cut the connection we have formed over the past thirty years.

Of all the times together we shared, our best ones were when we stayed the weekend with Grandma.

Both grandmas (on our mother's side and also on our father's side) lived nearby in our small town. As a way to distinguish between the two, I christened each grandma after the mice in the children's story *City Mouse, Country Mouse*. One grandma lived on a working farm and the other lived in town, so to remedy any confusion when announcing our next sleepover, why not appropriately label them "Country Grandma" and "City Grandma"? As labels tend to do, they stuck.

While I loved both grandmas equally, each sleepover presented different perks. At City Grandma's I knew I would be allowed to eat my two favorite food groups the entire weekend: baked potatoes and halved lemons covered in salt. (My mouth waters now just thinking about it.) A trip to Walmart would likely happen, and our scan at the checkout would include a sassy new pair of shoes for me, "just like Grandma's."

My brother and I would spend countless hours running around City Grandma's neighborhood, meeting each kid in a four-block radius while eating every Popsicle from the freezer. We would end each evening with an intriguing episode of *Murder, She Wrote* while perfecting our crocheting abilities on the couch next to City Grandma. I cherished our times in her home, and I wished for more of them each time we had to leave.

Now at Country Grandma's we had to follow more rules, but we had plenty of activities. However, we would not be allowed to eat junk food for three days straight—no way, José. We ate fresh from the garden. We helped cook the meals, and we ate them without grumbling. Anthony would check on the cows with Country Grandpa on the four-wheeler while I would snap peas into giant five-gallon buckets on the back porch with Country Grandma. Anthony and I both learned to sew, plant gardens, fish and jump hay bales.

We loved Country Grandma's house because, once we learned our territorial boundaries, we could run free. We hiked up the gravel road to the old cemetery on top of "Spook Hill." We pretended we were real-life Boxcar Children, lost and in search of our family. We decorated T-shirts with puff paints and had intense mud fights in the pond out back. We wrote and directed our own theatrical plays and performed them in the basement, charging a nickel from each family member we forced to attend. We put together puzzles and played solitaire on TV dinner tray tables while our grandparents watched the evening news.

Into adulthood we still jumped hay bales and went on walks up Spook Hill. Our love for our grandmas did not change when they moved to different homes or moved into new seasons of life. The passage of time only deepened our appreciation for the love they had showered on us in our formative years. They loved us as babies, as know-it-all fourth-graders, as smelly teens and as absentminded adults.

Great Expectations

Either Grandma's house was a sanctuary. My happy place, where my unbridled love for crafts could be made manifest. No one had to convince Anthony or me that time spent with City Grandma or Country Grandma would be awesome. As soon as we heard the words, "Slumber party at Grandma's tonight," we knew we were in for a treat, regardless of which one it was. We knew because we had been to our grandmas' houses before and we had had a blast each time. We knew what to expect: fun, fun and more fun.

Great expectations are at the heart of enthusiastic encounters.

This applies to our encounters with God, too. When we imagine spending time with God, our minds can take us in a number of directions, good and bad. Depending on your past experiences with faith and church, you may see religion as a punishment, more like *Weekend at Bernie's* than a weekend at Grandma's. When people talk about their relationship with God as "passionate" or "on fire," you may not identify in the least. You may feel discouraged because your faith does not get you excited. You may feel angry that other people get all God's love and attention at Walmart in the shoe department, while you are left walking through checkout with nothing special at all. It just is not fair that you have to work so hard at your relationship with Jesus.

May I ask you a personal question, just me to you? In your heart of hearts, what do you expect from your time with God? Do you enter into prayer expecting God to answer? Do you open your Bible expecting the words to jump off the page?

Are you expecting God to show up in a big way, either in your relationship or how you serve Him? Is your time spent with God exciting and fresh? Or do you believe that spiritual passion is a feeling you must achieve on your own? Do you expect to muscle your way into it, take it by force if necessary? If clicking your heels together fails to do the trick, do you assume that you will have to pray harder, pray longer, read your Bible more?

What does God have to say about this? "I will give them a heart to know me" (Jeremiah 24:7). He will give me what I need. A heart that longs for God is a gift from God Himself. Passionate faith must be given to me. I cannot pray harder or read longer to find it. I cannot manufacture it. The best Spotify worship music playlist cannot usher it in. I cannot make my prayers "cooler" or "better" to convince God I am worthy of His gift. He does not need me to spice it up, only to open up.

This is good news! I cannot create a passion for prayer and reading God's Word; I must *ask* for it. God is the giver of good gifts and passion is one of them. When Jesus died on the cross and rose again, He gave us complete access to every one of His gifts. Not a "guest" portion. Not some kind of a replica. God gives us everything He gives Christ—in full measure. There are no half-victories with Him, no partial healings, no still-shackled freedom. No sort-of redemption or halfhearted forgiveness. Jesus was fully raised from the dead and His victory is complete. His passion can be my passion! Thank You, Jesus, I do not have to do this alone.

And how can you and I access such an incredible power? By asking. That is the key.

This is why I love prayer.

I pray, *God, I want to desire You more than I do right now, but I don't know how. Will You give me the desire I cannot create myself?*

Be honest. What do you expect from God when you pray? Miracles, or status quo?

How often do we approach prayer with God with low expectations? "Good things do not happen for me. I do not get what I pray for as others do. This must be normal. I don't know why I should expect anything different."

Prayer becomes a powerless option, a method to use when there is no other option. "Since I can't really make a difference, I guess I will just pray." Faithless, we approach prayer with a ho-hum attitude, expecting nothing.

Shifting Focus

After I learned to trust that God would give me passion if I asked for it, I decided to sit back and watch for His goodness in action. I shifted my focus from how I lacked passion to how God was showing up in my life. In other words, I changed my orientation from myself to Him. I used to think, *Why is God not showing up for me?* Now my expectation changed: *God, I am waiting for You to show up.* My thought patterns were being reformed. I was learning to trust in His provision. I had been missing a deeper relationship with God because of my orphan mentality; I felt I had to provide for myself. Now I started taking Paul's advice. He told the people of the church: "Devote yourselves to prayer, being watchful and thankful" (Colossians 4:2). As a result of my expectant prayer, the possibilities have expanded without limits.

What if we asked God to show up big? I mean crazy, Bible-miracles big. When we shift our expectancy from blah to hoorah, we see God all around us. Watch for His goodness. Be thankful for increased spiritual passion in your life even before it has come to pass. Wait expectantly for Him to give you everything you need to live a life of godliness. Unless you stop walking through life expecting table scraps, that is exactly what you will get.

What about the Bible? Do you, like most people, wonder how anyone can be inspired to read all the words in the Bible, even the Old Testament law and those weird "begats"? I did. Then God gave me passion for His Word, and I could not get enough of it. As it turns out, the Bible is anything but boring. If we remain stuck in our opinion of His Word as dated and uninspired, then revelation will continue to elude us. But if we read the Bible with fresh eyes, hungry for new knowledge and fresh anointing, it will come to life.

The Bible is our constant source of communication from God, and He uses it to teach us all we need to know about the essentials of our faith. It becomes the filter through which we can strain every thought and situation.

Need more truth in your life? Open your Bible: "All Scripture is God-breathed and is useful for teaching, rebuking, correcting and training in righteousness" (2 Timothy 3:16).

The Bible is alive. It will respond to whatever situations you are currently walking in. The same section of Scripture can speak to ninety different dilemmas. That is insanely cool! The stories of heroic feats and romantic exploits keep you engaged and longing for the next part of the story. You can get lost in the lives of those who lived long ago but who endured the same types of circumstances you do today.

God's Word is constant. Its application is anything but out-of-date. You have a fresh word from God waiting each day. Do you see it? Are you willing to hold on to it as you wait for it to come to fruition in your life, no matter the cost?

When you lack passion, when you feel like you are going through the motions of prayer and Christianity, just stop. Stop trying to arm-wrestle God into letting you win. Instead, ask Him for passion. Ask Him for perseverance. Go from have-not to have. From empty to full. From adequate to excessive. You will find out that your enthusiasm for prayer is part of a much bigger plan.

The Overflow Valve

Passion overflows. Yes, God wants us to pursue an exciting relationship with Him, but that is not the only goal. God knows that if we have passion for what He is doing in our lives, we will tell others about it.

When we get excited about something, we tend to shout it from the rooftops. We seem to have been created to share. This need to connect with people about our passions has been knitted into our souls. That is why we tweet and post on Facebook about all the things we love—quotes, pictures of our dog, achievements, good books. So much more should we share about God. This is how He uses us to save a dying world.

Your light shines for the sake of others. The flame of your passion draws others to God. Jesus said so:

> You are the light of the world. A town built on a hill cannot be hidden. Neither do people light a lamp and put it under a bowl. Instead they put it on its stand, and it gives light to everyone in the house. In the same way, let your light shine before others, that they may see your good deeds and glorify your Father in heaven.
>
> Matthew 5:14–16

It is your God-given duty to seek the passion the Father provides and then to share it with the world. This is no small flicker you carry. It is a flame ignited by the power of heaven, the Spirit of the living God inside of you. Run with this torch as though your life and the lives of others depend on it, because they do.

The relationship you are finding in God is meant to set the world ablaze. Be a shining example of Christ in the words you speak and the life you live. Others are watching.

Your outlet may not be like mine: a blog or a book. But you have friends. You have family. You have your monthly coffee date with your book club. When you share this hope you have found with anyone you encounter, you will see that contagious passion guarantees effectiveness that is off the charts. People flock to Christ when passion overflows.

"That's great, Erica. I have been asking, but I get nada. What's wrong with me? Does God even hear me? I want passion and fire and I keep coming up empty."

What if you are asking for passion, yet you feel nothing? Are you ready to give up? How do you share a story with others that you do not have yourself?

You are not the only one to experience frustration in waiting on God to move in a mighty way. There are many examples of this in the Bible, but one of my favorites is the untold story of Priest Number Seven. Let me explain what I mean.

Parade of Priests

You may have sung the same song I did in elementary school, where white suburban children attempt to sing about the Bible story of Joshua and the walls of Jericho that came "a-tumblin' down." Hard as they tried, bless their hearts, our valiant music teachers never could pull an ounce of gospel-style soul out of us. But we did learn the Bible story.

We are all familiar with the story of Joshua and the battle of Jericho, but do you know what led up to that battle? The Israelites wandered in the desert for years until Joshua took charge after Moses. Moses was quite an act to follow. (I think of him as the Vin Diesel of the Bible. After all, that dude saw God in the form of fire, confronted Pharaoh to his face, and then did a mean Tokyo drift into the Red Sea and it divided. If Moses were alive today, he would be wearing a too-small tank and racing bad guys around the streets of L.A.)

I would not want to be the guy trying to fill Moses' shoes after he died, would you? But Joshua had his faith on his side. He was one of the original men who had been sent to spy out the land for the Israelites, one of only two who came back with a report that God would conquer the land he had promised them, no matter the obstacles that stood in their way. Joshua was a man who understood the power of following God.

He was faithful when no one else was, and now God was promoting him to Guy in Charge over the Israelites. To be sure, they were hard to love and hard to lead. God must have given Joshua a special supernatural love for those whiners.

When the time had come to conquer the Promised Land, Joshua sent spies ahead to check it out before he went into battle. Then we read the famous story of Rahab the prostitute hiding the spies on her rooftop patio and receiving a promise of safety in return. The spies returned and passed the good news on to Joshua: "It's go time."

God had promised His people that they would take the city as their own, but they would have to be obedient to follow God's direction in every detail. The men may have had grand visions of sword fights with the *Rocky* theme song playing in their ears as they cut down the competition. Destroying a city is never pretty. Then Joshua presented God's grand plan of attack:

"God said to have a parade of priests lead us around the city for seven days, and on the seventh day the walls surrounding the city will come a-tumblin' down. This is going to be awesome. You seven priests are leading the way. Good luck. Everyone in on 'Holy Parade'—1, 2, 3 . . . *Holy Parade*."

I can see the wheels turning in the minds of the army as Joshua revealed the strategy. They had to be scrambling for an explanation of what they had just heard: *We are going to walk around a wall? A parade will conquer a city? All right. Maybe we should make it a scary parade with, like, big inflatable clowns that look evil. That could work, maybe. What if we throw some kind of really gross candy that no one likes, like stale Tootsie Rolls? Yes, then they would know this isn't normal parade and we mean business.*

Here is the Bible version, in case you feel I have taken a few liberties:

> Now the gates of Jericho were securely barred because of the Israelites. No one went out and no one came in. Then the Lord said to Joshua, "See, I have delivered Jericho into your hands, along with its king and its fighting men. March around the city once with all the armed men. Do this for six days. Have seven priests carry trumpets of rams' horns in front of the ark. On the seventh day, march around the city seven times, with the priests blowing the trumpets. When you hear them sound a long blast on the trumpets, have the whole army give a loud shout; then the wall of the city will collapse and the army will go up, everyone straight in."
>
> Joshua 6:1–5

See? It is a parade. You can imagine Priest Number Seven was in shock. His job, along with Priests Number One through Six, was to lead an entire people group into battle with no personal protection. They were to walk (as macho as possible) around a wall that was indestructible. I bet at that point he was wishing he was lucky Priest Number Eight who had dodged the holy draft that day. *Priest Bob has all the luck.* . . .

God was speaking to Joshua, not to Priest Number Seven. He was not the one receiving God's revelation; Joshua was. Being a priest for the nation of Israel could not have been an easy job to begin with, and now it had just become harder. He was supposed to trust that God was speaking this crazy plan to Joshua and then to follow the plan without question.

How hard is it for us to follow God when we cannot hear Him, when we question His supposed guidance? This priest did not have a direct line to God himself because Jesus had not yet paved the way. Number Seven was living pre-Cross, which meant the Holy Spirit was not directing him from the inside.

All he could see was a big wall that stood between him and God's promise, and apparently it was his job to usher in the next miracle that God had for His people. What would he do? Contradict Joshua? Persuade his fellow priests to boycott the whole crazy scheme? Or would he choose to trust God's promise and persevere? Around and around the wall for seven days. Seven days of questioning if they had all lost their minds. Seven days of wondering where God was in all the mess. Seven priests, seven horns, seven days, seven circles etched out by their feet as they walked round and round.

You may feel like Priest Number Seven, blindly trusting in God's promises as you pray for passion, begging for the power of God to rise up in your heart in a new way, praying and pacing round and round. God has promised to give you passion, but you are not feeling it. You are not hearing Him. Trying to believe what His Word says, you find yourself in an endless parade. Round and round, asking and asking, trusting and trusting.

You are tired of going in circles. When will the walls of your Jericho fall? When will your passion ignite?

Victory is coming, rest assured. Your faithfulness will bring your promise to fruition, just as it did when the priests and the army trusted Joshua and ultimately, God. Your walls will come down and you will take the city. Promise.

Keep On Keepin' On

God will give you all you need when you need it, but it may take a minute to get in sync with Him. We want passion, but we would like it to look a certain way. We think of passion as an outward expression of delight and excitement. We expect it to feel good. What if God ignites your passion by means of a rough patch in your marriage? Or what if you are already an outwardly expressive person, and God shows up in your quiet, isolated moments with Him, the exact opposite of what you anticipated?

Why does it not happen for you as it has for everyone else? In your times of waiting and worrying, be patient. Keep calm. Do not take matters into your own hands, flinging dishes or storming the castle. God is never late. And you are never more prepared to receive His passion than in those unlikely moments. Even when you are bored out of your mind in another church service or prayer meeting where you feel nothing and see nothing, God is near to you. He has not forgotten you. He will never turn His back on you.

Keep on keeping on, praying through thick and thin. Look what Scripture advises:

> Never be lacking in zeal, but keep your spiritual fervor, serving the Lord. Be joyful in hope, patient in affliction, patient in prayer.
>
> Romans 12:11–12

Drop the mic. Is this saying that as I pursue God for more passion, I must do it with passion? That I need to show some enthusiasm? That I may run into roadblocks that require extra patience? That it may not go as I plan? Yes. And God knew this would happen, which is why He wrote you these reminders.

All I can bring is my surrender. He brings what He wants to bring. I have to be okay with the way He gives me His gifts. I cannot be angry that today's prayer does not "feel like" yesterday's prayer, or blame the church that I do not hear God when I read my Bible. There are an overwhelming number of barriers that make up our personal Jericho walls.

All I can tell you is: "Show up."

Show up. Every day. Over and over. Do not give up or give in. Keep your eyes on the prize and keep coming. God will not let you down. Not every early-morning prayer produces fruit immediately. There have been weeks when I have pressed in and pressed in, only to hear crickets. I have read through entire books of the Bible and not remembered a single word I read.

Just show up, and do not stop showing up.

My new motto: Diligence is essential to divine discovery.

God is on your side. He is never as silent as you fear. Do not get discouraged in the journey—He is holding your hand through it all.

Check Your Pulse

1. Describe what passion means to you.

2. When was a time you felt excited to read God's Word or pray? How did it differ from the times you were not excited? How did it change your interaction with God?

3. In your circle of friends which ones would you say are enthusiastic about God? How do you see that spill over onto others?

4. What holds you back from sharing God's movement in your life with those you encounter? How can you be bold in telling your story to others?

5. If you are waiting for passion to manifest itself in your life, trust that it is coming. Keep asking. Keep pressing in. Ask God what He wants to say to you in this season of waiting.

PART TWO

GOD'S PERFECT TRUTH

five

Satan Is a Jerk

A cool breeze, a small shovel, and fingernails caked with fresh soil. This holy trinity can only mean one thing: Spring has sprung.

Azaleas, hydrangeas, cannas, iris and tulip. Each flower is unique in fragrance and display, and together they bring beauty to a barren world. Flowers are "just because," and that frivolousness makes me love them all the more. I welcome the worthy work that is required to produce a long season of colorful blooms that I can see from my kitchen window. It is good to be a gardener.

After a gardening day, I greet the morning, coffee cup in hand, as I inspect my tidy flower bed, pleased with the results. And then I see it. A weed. Smack dab in the middle of my perfect garden. *How dare you!*

Last night when I left my precious petal babies there were no cursed weeds anywhere to be found. Now less than twelve hours later, invaders have arrived. I know the truth about those weeds from my years of experience: One weed can take over an entire garden. Weeds spread like gangrene and choke out the good plants.

Not here, you trespasser! I yank that sucker right out of the ground and toss in in the weed pile. Breathe fresh, little ones. Mama Erica is on the watch.

The Sneaky Gardener

Satan wants nothing more than to claim the garden of my heart as his own. He is a gardener of sorts. He will invade this fragile garden if I let him, reshaping the landscape as he sees fit. A little lie here, a frustration there, a border of brightly colored abuse and past regrets. He will distort the way I view God and how I see myself. He will try to disqualify me from my calling. He may enter my garden and plant only one tiny lie. But that one seed, if not spotted and yanked out, will grow into a weed that can choke out the truth that God sowed into my heart when He created me.

The devil is continually looking for ways to ruin each one of us. (See 1 Peter 5:8.) His job is to destroy everything good and lovely and pure. He targets our thoughts, our godly discipline, our contentment. A happy marriage and family can bring out the worst in him. He tempts and taunts and whispers lies. He sows doubts about God's unconditional love. He undermines victories over strongholds. Satan refutes our unique gifts and our God-given purpose.

We are not the first to feel the sting of Satan's schemes. This fallen world started in another time and place, in a Garden full of promise. That is, until the sneaky snake entered the picture. Our story begins with those fig-leaf-clad images of the father and mother of all mess-ups: Adam and Eve. Their gardens were lush and beautiful, but they did not pay attention to God's instructions to them as the caretakers. The enemy's seeds took root all too easily. Genesis 3:1–7 tells the story.

> Now the serpent was more crafty than any of the wild animals the LORD God had made. He said to the woman, "Did God really say, 'You must not eat from any tree in the garden'?" The woman said to the serpent, "We may eat fruit from the trees in the garden, but God did say, 'You must not eat fruit from the tree that is in the middle of the garden, and you must not touch it, or you will die.'"
>
> "You will not certainly die," the serpent said to the woman. "For God knows that when you eat from it your eyes will be opened, and you will be like God, knowing good and evil." When the woman saw that the fruit of the tree was good for food and pleasing to the eye, and also desirable for gaining wisdom, she took some and ate it. She also gave some to her husband, who was with her, and he ate it. Then the eyes of both of them were opened, and they realized they were naked; so they sewed fig leaves together and made coverings for themselves."

Satan did what he does best: He planted a seed of doubt, sprinkled a little water, and stood back to watch it grow. Essentially, he was saying to Eve, "God is a liar. God is withholding. God is not as smart as you."

Satan's name badge reads Liar, and he wears it still today. His old lies fasten themselves in our minds and hearts:

"Did God really tell you that you are chosen? Beautiful? Redeemed?"

"God has better things for you, but He is keeping them for Himself. You had better take control."

"You are so gifted and smart. Why are you listening to God? He is treating you like a slave. Don't you want to be truly free?"

Eve did not know that the serpent's promise of freedom would lead only to enslavement. The fruit was beautiful and the reasoning sounded convincing, so she fell into slavery with her first bite. The enemy always tells us that if we toss God's instruction to the side we will be smarter, stronger and happier. Satan twists the truth 180 degrees, telling us that freedom in Christ is slavery.

Romans 6:20–23 describes true freedom in Christ:

> When you were slaves to sin, you were free from the control of righteousness. What benefit did you reap at that time from the things you are now ashamed of? Those things result in death! But now that you have been set free from sin and have become slaves of God, the benefit you reap leads to holiness, and the result is eternal life. For the wages of sin is death, but the gift of God is eternal life in Christ Jesus our Lord.

What did Adam and Eve reap by believing Satan's lies? Death. Not only for themselves, but for all human beings. Eating from the tree was an outward expression of an inner mistrust. Like Eve, we all question, "Can I really trust God?" That second-guessing causes us to take control and make decisions without God. Doubt keeps us from believing boldly.

Believing the Lie

Satan sneaks into your glorious garden with this debilitating lie: You are not who God says you are. "You are no good at being you. You should be someone else. Someone prettier, smarter, more successful. You are not as great as He claims you are."

That one lie, believed to the core, kills us all.

I know the struggle all too well. I, too, used to desperately attempt to be someone else. She is cool and funny. She is more patient and loving than I. She is the perfect balance of submitted to God yet driven to achieve her goals. She makes it to the gym when she should. She cooks amazing meals. She is talented yet humble, gentle yet strong. She never speaks out of turn or hurts others. She is all things light and sweet and adventurous. She is perfect.

I have spent years chasing this perfect girl, only to realize that she is not real. She does not exist. I cannot see her face nor can I wrap my arms around her. She is only a figment of my imagination created from the best characteristics of every woman I have known. Every day I tried to make myself resemble her a little more closely. This perfect version of myself became my idol. Now I lovingly refer to her as Perfectica, the ugly stepsister of the real Erica. (It was the coolest superhero name I could think of. Cut me some slack.)

Every decision filtered through W.W.P.D.: "What Would Perfectica Do?"

My brain went into overdrive: *Am I doing everything right? Do I measure up? What if I fail?*

When I thought of all the ways I fell short, I became an anxious waterfall of emotions spilling over an edge far too high for me to navigate. My thoughts swirled together in a pool of perfect hesitation as I continually wondered about the "right" way to do it all. I wanted to hit the target, make the grade, land the part. If I did not? I had better get back to work until I did.

Perfectionism. It will steal your identity and cripple your calling.

I wrongly believed that following Jesus would make me perfect. Yet I never looked like Perfectica. My house was always too messy. My gym schedule revolved around needing a break from my kids, not caring for my health. My mouth got me in trouble, the frustrations of a long day boiling over on my husband and kids in unkind words and deep sighs. I prayed, but not enough. I read my Bible but never memorized it. I cared about the earth but I failed to recycle every empty bottle. I even felt guilty for watching a movie. *Perfectica would never waste time on a movie when a pile of clothing waits to be folded.*

Perfectica was in charge. My purpose and hope were placed on her approval, not Christ's. I never looked to Jesus to validate my successes or disapprove my failures; Perfectica did it for me. I did not bow down to a golden calf or bronze Buddha. I was not even worshiping myself. I was worshiping the "me I could be." Worshiping anything besides God is idolatry and I was in deep. The image of my perfect self received all my accolades and attention, my time and my talents. Perfectica was a false god and I had put her above the true God.

I know I am not alone. I know others also feel the pull to measure up and make the grade. Your perfect image may look nothing like mine, but it haunts you just the same.

The lies of an idol grow more insistent. Our best can never satisfy. I was falling short daily, yet Perfectica kept pushing me to achieve. She was always looking to the next outcome, never settling for second place, never applauding effort. Somehow I believed if I tried hard enough and stuck with it long enough, with enough self-discipline, I would eventually gaze into the mirror and see Perfectica staring back. A goddess among women.

Yet every time I looked, the reflection fell short. I wasted years trying to satisfy the opinions of an imaginary girl. Whatever I attempted, Perfectica would stand over me wagging a finger, "Shame, shame. You can do better."

Geez, Perfectica. You are kind of a jerk. For real.

You know who else is a jerk? Satan.

Satan Is a Jerk

Satan knows that effective members of the kingdom of God must fully believe in their value and calling. Whenever he can plant doubts about a person's worth, gifting, value or purpose, he wins. His goal is to cripple Christians and to interfere with the healthy growth of the kingdom of God.

Satan was the first one to plant the lie that I was not good enough. It set a course for my life that was dominated by performance and restlessness. Satan knows my story all too well because it is his own.

Satan began as Lucifer, a commander of the angels. He was gorgeous, smart and powerful. I would call him the tall, dark and handsome of the angelic world. He had it going on.

Until he questioned his identity. Lucifer, instead of accepting who he was created to be, rejected the purpose for which God had shaped him and went looking for greener pastures. Lucifer believed he was better than God.

He felt he should be in charge. He knew God would not go for an exchange of positions, so he decided to take the throne by force. The book of Isaiah describes the devil's transition from Lucifer to Satan:

> How you have fallen from heaven, morning star, son of the dawn! You have been cast down to the earth, you who once laid low the nations! You said in your heart, "I will ascend to the heavens; I will raise my throne above the stars of God; I will sit enthroned on the mount of assembly, on the utmost heights of Mount Zaphon. I will ascend above the tops of the clouds; I will make myself like the Most High." But you are brought down to the realm of the dead, to the depths of the pit.
>
> Isaiah 14:12–15

Lucifer did not keep his sin to himself. The talk at the water cooler became, "Did you hear? Lucifer beat God arm wrestling last night. God isn't as powerful as He claims to be." Lucifer was persuasive enough to convince one-third of the angels to rebel against God. One-third! I have met some sweet talkers in my day, but this is extreme. He cunningly convinced them that he should indeed be the guy on the throne. He used the very gifts God had given him to assert himself against the Giver, perverting the power and influence he had been given.

Satan is still taking the gifts of God and distorting them for his own purpose. He sows division, discouragement, mistrust and pride. The gardens of our hearts are still poisoned by the fruit that tempted Eve so long ago.

God sent Jesus to remove the poison still running in our veins, through His death on the cross. Our part is to repent of the lies we have believed and to find out who God says we are. Even though people have been getting it wrong for thousands of years, He has made it possible to trust Him.

God Renames Us

Satan rejected his own identity and he will exhaust himself to destroy ours. Every day he told me that I would never measure up so I may as well give up. Lucifer tried to rename himself King of Kings. I renamed myself Perfectica—Perfect Enough. What are you attempting to rename yourself?

Good Enough? Pretty Enough? Smart Enough? Holy Enough?

We shape our identity around our names, like it or not. Our money, time and hearts get entangled in trying to compensate for what we lack. The fact that acceptance, love and holiness in the eyes of God cannot be purchased or earned does not compute well in our human brains. We cannot believe God has truly equipped us with all we need. If we do not feel beautiful enough, we buy the skin cream that claims to improve our looks. Our callings may stretch us beyond what we know how to do, so we kill ourselves trying to "figure it out." We believe God is withholding the secret formula for success in all areas of life.

Only after God renamed me could I defeat the lies.

I no longer needed to strive for a seat at the table. I learned that my value lies in the name God gives me and not the one I so desperately tried to claim. I found out that God has a better name for me. He has a better name for you, too. He calls you Chosen. Beautiful. Precious. Loved. Forgiven.

Your true identity is not you, perfect. It is you, perfected.

God created you to be *you*. He did not create you to be your neighbor or your friend. He put you together, every detail and unique characteristic carefully thought out: your smile, your voice, your deep love for intentional connection, whatever makes you you. He fashioned you from the dust into something beautiful. He placed you in this time and space in eternity for a reason. He names you as He sees you and His vision is perfect.

God is a professional Namer. Your name carries your identity and He knows you better than you know yourself. God delights in renaming us. He changed Abram's name to Abraham and Sarai to Sarah with a promise of children when they had none. He gave Saul, the persecutor of Christ-followers, a new name at his conversion—Paul. Simon was named Peter shortly after becoming one of Jesus' twelve disciples.

By renaming us, God reverses our unbelief, our sinful nature and our adulterous hearts. He turns them into faithful, clean, loyal hearts. The names He gives us match the identities He assigns. He sees past the yuck and reclaims your true identity. God does not reject your old name—He redeems it. You were once Lost; now you are Found. Once Rejected, now Accepted. Once Dead, now Alive.

I no longer have to become Perfectica, because Erica is all I need to be. Instead of creating a new version of myself, I need only embrace who God says I am. What name does God have waiting for you?

All in a Name

My ministry is called Believe Boldly, but rarely do I feel bold. I have found that being bold is much different than I envisioned. I used to picture myself bravely standing in front of crowds, shouting out the truth of God's love and redemption with passion and energy. While those moments do happen occasionally, I have worked out much of my boldness through trembling and tears, when "brave" seemed a million miles away. Being bold means becoming who God created you to be, even when it is scary or painful.

For a while, this apparent contradiction caused me to question my identity. I had named my ministry Believe Boldly, but was that true about me? Did I trust in God with boldness, or was I a poser? The enemy planted doubt in my heart. *Am I the person God says I am? Am I bold?*

Then out of my circle of friends came words of truth. Five women who had no idea how I was struggling spoke boldness over me.

"Thank you for your boldness. It is an inspiration."

"Your willingness to speak out has changed me. Thank you for being bold."

"I was ready to run out, but you stayed strong. You are so bold."

Their words should have taken care of everything, but my mind and the enemy worked as a dynamic duo to block the truth by arguing it away: *They only say that because they are my friends and want to encourage me, not because it is true. . . . Subconsciously they link me with being bold because of the blog. I'm not bold the way I should be. . . . Just because talking about Jesus is less scary for me than for other people doesn't make me bold. It just means I am a loudmouth.*

I know I am not the only one who does this. We all argue away the truth in exchange for the counterfeit. But God was not done with me. He was determined to speak my true identity over me. At our local women's Bible study later that week, I sat at the back of the room pondering my friends' words versus the words of the enemy.

Am I bold, God? Am I who You say I am? The way I have been serving You hasn't felt bold. It is terrifying to do what You ask. I don't feel indestructible or reassured. I am confused about what bold means.

At the end of the study another friend, Shanda, found me at the back of the room. She was holding a mason jar with colorful papers inside. She explained that as she had prepared to lead her small group for the Bible study, God had given her a list of identity words to share with her group. Each woman was supposed to pull from the jar and receive the "random" word God had for them. It had been a wonderful evening around her table. As the women had selected the words, each one turned out to have special meaning for that particular woman. Afterward, my friend realized she had extra words in her jar.

"God said to give you one of these words," she said. I eagerly agreed to take one. I love when God speaks to me through unique methods. I excitedly reached into the jar and grabbed one of the slips of paper. What do you think that paper said?

"BOLD."

Of all the words given and with all of the women who had already pulled words from the jar, God had reserved this one for me. There was no denying it. God was saying I was bold, regardless if I felt it or believed it myself. He would declare it over me in spoken words, written notes, songs and even the Bible until I would allow it to become my truth. My new name.

What is God declaring over you that you refuse to believe? What are you gifted to accomplish that you shy away from? It is easy to hide from the hard things, but I want to challenge you to be who you are created to be, even when you are scared. Embracing the identity that God gives us is true freedom.

Finding Freedom

One day my daughter Reese woke earlier than usual. She emerged from her room, hair messy from her pillow, and jumped into my arms. It is our morning snuggle ritual. She complains about my bad breath and I squeeze her in a bear hug that is a little too strong. It is the best start to the day.

Her heart's desire for that day? Immediate baking.

"Mom, can we make cupcakes right now? I want them so bad! Can we, please?"

She is 100 percent her father's daughter.

"Honey, it is incredibly early for cupcakes. Maybe we should make them after lunch."

Her face was despondent. Oh, that face . . .

Very clearly, I heard the Holy Spirit speak to me: *Says who? Who says it is too early for cupcakes?*

Says who? Well God, everybody. Everyone agrees that cupcakes for breakfast are irresponsible.

Actually, no. Come to think of it, no one has ever spoken that to me. Where did I get this rule? Where did I get *all* these rules? Be organized. Be punctual. Be the perfect mom. Be the woman whose own needs never matter. Be the superhero who does not need God to accomplish anything.

Perfectica had been running amok my entire life and I was finally recognizing it. No person had given me rules or fed me these lies. It was only my ridiculous idol of perfection. I was done trying to meet her standards. That image of my perfect self had been in charge for long enough. No longer would she cripple me from being *myself*.

I snatched up my little girl and we marched straight to the kitchen, where we made the most glorious mess we have ever made. It was free and silly and absolutely perfect in the eyes of God.

And fresh cupcakes are divine for breakfast.

Check Your Pulse

1. When you were growing up, how did the enemy plant seeds of doubt and untruth in your mind and heart? How has that shaped the way you see yourself today?

2. Do you have any idols in your life right now? Ask God to reveal what you may be worshiping besides Him.

3. How have others, including even Satan, mislabeled you? How have those lies shaped your current identity?

4. If you could be any kind of person, who would you be? How does that line up with your true identity?

5. God wants to reveal a new you. Sit quietly, close your eyes, and ask Him to give you an image of the true you.

six

Armor Up

My ears caught her cry.

"Mama! Mama! Look at me!"

It was only the one thousandth "Mama!" I had heard in the past five minutes, so I coolly ignored it.

"Mama! Mama!"

"Maaaaaa-maaaaaaa!!!"

"What, Reese?"

I turned to see her disgusted face, bright blue dye rubbed along her lip line. She was spitting out something she did not like the taste of. What? She held up a small white package covered in the same blue substance.

Rat Poison.

"Oh no! Reese! Spit it out! Oh no . . . Oh no! How much did you eat?" My questions were not answered with coherent words from my toddler, so I stuck my finger in her mouth and began pulling out pieces of blue crystal meant to kill a small animal. My heart beating rapidly in my chest, I called 911.

"No, I don't know how much she ate. . . . Yes, she is breathing okay. . . . No, I don't know the address here." The answers poured out of my mouth faster than my mind could form them.

That rat poison had come from a storage unit. Our church did not have a permanent building, so we kept many of our supplies there. My serving as a children's pastor while also being a stay-at-home mom meant that I had to bring Reese with me when I went to the storage unit. While I worked, I was letting her run the hallway outside of the unit. Back and forth, she ran and laughed. It was a great solution to keep her busy and happy . . . until it was not.

Waiting for a fire truck and ambulance to pull into the empty parking lot in the back of the storage building, Reese was acting completely normal and laughing carelessly. I was a hot ball of sweat and nerves, beating myself up with Mom Guilt.

How could I have been so stupid? Why did I not think to check for rat poison in the storage unit? I had no idea it was even there.

My internal wrestling match dinged the end of the round when the paramedics arrived and checked Reese's vitals. She was acting normal and her blood pressure was perfect. She would be fine, praise God. The men who came to our rescue took time to calm my fears with an explanation of how that particular rat poison was designed to work.

They told me that the substance was made to be fatal to a small animal, but that it would not kill immediately. In fact, it would take dose after dose to slowly shut down the animal's internal organs and bring about death. While other poisons work much faster and are more lethal, the kind Reese swallowed would leave her with no side effects. For her to have serious internal damage, she would need to ingest very large amounts over several days. What she had just swallowed did not hurt her in the slightest.

This is so much like the poison of temptation and sin. Ingested repeatedly over time, it can kill.

An attack from the enemy is poison. Sin, when first offered, tastes bitter and we may even spit it out. But over time we become calloused to the bitterness and keep eating. We believe the devil and take in all he has to offer, ignorant that we are eating our way to our death because of all that poison.

What are we thinking? Why are we choosing to die a slow painful death devoid of God's victory? Sure, Satan cannot steal our ultimate salvation, but he can make our time on earth a living hell if we let him.

The Battle Is Real

We are surrounded by an invisible world, populated with both good guys and bad guys.

> For by him all things were created, in heaven and on earth, visible and invisible, whether thrones or dominions or rulers or authorities—all things were created through him and for him.
>
> Colossians 1:16 ESV

The angels that work for God are the good guys. Satan and his demons are the bad guys. Our job is to stick with the good guys and fight the bad. This is not an imaginary battle; it is real and we feel the effects of it daily. In fact, you could say that war is being waged for your soul every day in an invisible realm.

We must grasp some important truths if we are ever to win the war. For example: "You, dear children, are from God and have overcome them, because the one who is in you is greater than the one who is in the world" (1 John 4:4).

Jesus overcame the devil, therefore so will you. Satan cannot defeat you. When you make Jesus Lord of your life, you become

His child. His children inherit everything He has to offer, which includes victory over death and the devil. You will win every battle if you let God have total control of your heart and you walk in the fullness of His power.

We are armed and ready to fight, not with swords and guns and bombs, but rather with prayer and self-discipline:

> For though we live in the world, we do not wage war as the world does. The weapons we fight with are not the weapons of the world. On the contrary, they have divine power to demolish strongholds. We demolish arguments and every pretension that sets itself up against the knowledge of God, and we take captive every thought to make it obedient to Christ.
>
> 2 Corinthians 10:3–5

Your mind, kept alert and ready, can stop the voice of the enemy. Your words have the power to break strongholds of addiction and abuse. By capturing every thought and being obedient to what God says, not Satan, you will win every time.

We all have days that make us want to crawl back in bed and press the restart button. The alarm goes off late, the kids are moving at a snail's pace and your car runs out of gas on the way to school. While you call for help, you hear a puking sound from the backseat. . . .

Now you can chalk every one of those events up to the work of Satan and get upset, or you can ask for wisdom from the Holy Spirit. While it is true that a war is being waged against us, not every difficult circumstance represents the work of the enemy. Being too lazy to fill the car with gas before the gauge hit "E" is not a spiritual attack; it is a dumb choice. Less-than-stellar choices warrant consequences that are not enjoyable, but that does not indicate that they are all the work of Satan. Going to bed too late, forgetting to set an alarm, not being prepared for the day—these are not attacks. Our own free will gets us in trouble as much as temptation from the enemy can.

Now, sickness can absolutely be a spiritual attack. Getting rear-ended in your car can be, too. But how you react? The truth is that our mistakes and lack of responsibility are often like baiting the water for a shark attack. Satan jumps on every opportunity to provoke and heighten an emotional reaction. While your kids' lack of hustle may not be a spiritual attack, the temptation to lash out and scream until they move a millisecond faster is.

Satan offers a tempting selection of reactions: "Kids are annoying. Why not yell at them? My loudmouth reaction will make you feel much better."

"Your husband isn't helping around the house? I have a lovely Silent Treatment reaction you could sample. It's so gratifying."

"Lost your job? Poor you—what about some Self-Pity-Filled Depression for tonight? You know you deserve it."

We just react, forgetting all about the battle. We know we are fighting an invisible enemy and we know we have the power to disable his attacks, but we concede defeat instead. Instead of grabbing the package of poison and throwing it as far as possible, we sample and taste the reactions that look best.

After all, playing the victim is kind of delicious.

As victims we are not held responsible for our actions. We can blame everyone else. Instead of fighting back, victims can throw their hands up in defeat. Satan knows how tempting being a victim can be, so he whispers in your ear that you will never best him at his tricks. He convinces you that you are powerless. This does not start out having much of a hold on you, but then it does. Satan goes for the kill shot every time, and you need to be ready to block him, ninja style.

Ninjas

Being a ninja in our family is akin to walking on water. If my children believe you are a true ninja, you are automatically elevated to a level of cool that no one else can obtain.

For years we had them convinced that my brother, Anthony, was a ninja. Every time he came over, my son Tristan would plead for a "new move" so he could beat up any bad guys that might attack him in the grocery store or on the playground. Anthony always gave him a new kick or a special hold to try, but none was as powerful as Sneakiness. Tristan's favorite ninja technique was entering a room undetected. Oh, the power of being invisible! He could even spy on Mom and Dad's conversations.

Tristan invested his heart in mastering Sneakiness. Tiptoe here, belly-crawl there. There was not a room he could not enter undetected, at least in his own mind. The funny thing is he never knew what to do once he got into the room. He basically stood there and smiled at me until I turned around and jumped at the sight of him. That was all he needed to feel like a true ninja.

Now that he is older, he is not only sneaky, but terribly good at it. I am genuinely caught off guard sometimes when I turn around and he is standing there. I jump, yell and sometimes swing in his direction when I see him. He laughs hysterically and declares, "I totally scared you," while walking away.

I am not as amused by his accomplishment. We have had several talks about boundaries. We cannot have children sneaking into rooms randomly and unannounced, for heaven's sake.

Now Satan is a ninja, too, and when we first start to identify his attacks, they seem pretty lame. He sneaks into our lives with big ol' stomping footsteps, not sneaky at all. He thinks we are not smart enough to win the fight, so he picks easy and obvious attack methods. He is like a sloppy ninja and we can see and hear him coming every time. Your car breaks down. Your spouse is causing stress at home. The kids are rebelling. These are all so obvious. The enemy takes his aim at you, but he can afford to be sloppy and bumbling because you are such a new Christian. He does not consider you a true threat.

After time passes and you are still standing your ground, he knows you mean business. He refines his methods. He will enter the battle undetected, sword drawn. Before you know it, you find yourself engaged in a battle you were not expecting nor were you training for. This is like hand-to-hand combat. After a few go-rounds you start to gain traction. You need to train right in the thick of the battle in order to develop the skills and battle instincts that will serve you in the future.

Battle Plan

Every war needs an effective battle plan. No one shows up on the field to fight without knowing who the enemy is, what they are fighting for and the best fighting method for winning.

Where spiritual battles are concerned, God gives us all we need to know in the Bible. We need to know that (1) our enemy is the devil; (2) we are fighting for the salvation of others and the freedom that is promised to all Christians; (3) the best way to win is to "armor up" before going into the war.

Each piece of God's armor has a particular purpose, and we can read about it in the book of Ephesians:

> Therefore put on the full armor of God, so that when the day of evil comes, you may be able to stand your ground, and after you have done everything, to stand. Stand firm then, with the belt of truth buckled around your waist, with the breastplate of righteousness in place, and with your feet fitted with the readiness that comes from the gospel of peace. In addition to all this, take up the shield of faith, with which you can extinguish

all the flaming arrows of the evil one. Take the helmet of salvation and the sword of the Spirit, which is the word of God. And pray in the Spirit on all occasions with all kinds of prayers and requests. With this in mind, be alert and always keep praying for all the saints.

Ephesians 6:13–18

Let's break down the pieces. The belt of truth is the truth God teaches us about who He is and who we are. The breastplate of righteousness protects our hearts and reminds us of our right standing with God. The sandals of peace allow us to bring peace to any situation we face. The shield of faith gives us powerful protection from the enemy and any arrows he shoots at us. The helmet of salvation protects our minds from the words of Satan and reminds us that nothing can take us from God's hand; we are eternally His and have no need to fear. The sword of the Spirit is the Bible, with which we can distinguish the difference between God's word and the enemy's and then cut down any adversary.

I begin each day by "praying on" the armor of God. I envision putting on each piece and I declare aloud what it does. I want the enemy to know that I am ready for him and that he will not be able to sneak up on me without my knowledge. I declare that I will be faithful and filled with God's Word throughout my day, that I will not lose my temper or my resolve in the face of an enemy attack. I affirm that I will remain strong in the battle because I know who I am and Whose I am.

This Is a Family Fight

Your armor is never more important to have on than when the battle reaches your front doorstep. You have an important role to play in the spiritual protection of your family, and you must be diligent to keep the enemy at bay. Your boldness is vital. (I believe most of us would freak out if we could see what was happening behind the thin veil that separates us from the spiritual world. Evil is not pretty.)

Paige Henderson, co-founder of Fellowship of the Sword Ministries, once preached a message I will never forget. She referred to women as the "window" of their families because they have been gifted by God with a foreknowledge of the enemy's attacks, almost as if they are looking out of a high window. This explains why women tend to be the voice of warning in a family. They have been created to stand in the gap spiritually for their families, watchful against the attacks of the enemy and prepared to take spiritual authority over their domains. While the man is the head of the family, she is queen of the castle, and nothing dangerous gets over the moat when she is on the lookout.

I had struggled my whole married life to find my place under the leadership of my husband. I was never comfortable with submission, but I was also not thrilled with being in charge. Submission felt equal to silence, and I am anything but. What was I supposed to do with all these strong personality traits and passions that others have told me were a sign of pride? After hearing Paige's message, I finally knew my role. Submitting to my husband's authority did not take away any of my power to serve God as He had called me. It enhanced it.

With my husband covering our family during battle, I was free to watch from my spiritual window to identify the enemy's next step. Our teamwork would be the best defense against an attack. When I had not accepted my role in the family as lookout, I had left our family unguarded; the enemy could enter whenever he wanted. If I was busy trying to make the decisions reserved for my husband, our chain of command would falter. So I started to let the king shoulder his own role while I grew in owning mine. Together, we made our home impenetrable.

What did my new responsibilities look like? Under submission to my husband, I prayed over every room of my home, asking God for peace and protection. I also prayed that the enemy would have no authority or place in my home. The power I held as a Christian was not a new concept to me, so I prayed with boldness—aloud (the best way I knew how to fight an invisible battle). I prayed over my son's pillows and bed, that he would no longer have bad dreams. I did the same in my daughter's room. Down the hall, the kitchen, my office, even the back porch. I prayed for my marriage as I entered my own bedroom, my hands brushing over pillows and blankets as I asked God for sweet sleep and for our hearts to grow more in unity.

I did it again the next day. And the next. I took five minutes at the beginning of my day to walk through my home and set up a spiritual parameter. *Ain't nobody gonna break down my door on my watch.* Right away I began to notice a shift in my home. Everyone was happier. There was less fighting between siblings. We all slept soundly. My son's bad dreams completely stopped. But it did not end there.

My daughter began to pretend-play in ways I had never seen. Previously when she and I had played with her Barbie dolls, she usually acted out the same drama: Barbie slips and falls, Ken rescues her and they drive away in the Barbie car, only to fall off another cliff and need to be rescued again. Over and over, for hours, we fell off cliffs and rescued damsels in distress. Yet, after I had prayed over her room every morning for a week, our playtime changed. This time was different. This time Barbie fell off the cliff with no one to save her. After she hit the bottom, her Barbie friend came and embraced her with one hand extended to the sky. Reese sat there quietly for quite some time as she held the dolls in their extended hug. Curious at this new play, I asked, "What are they doing, Reese?"

"Well, this Barbie is praying for the other Barbie to be okay."

"That is very sweet of her. It is good to pray for our friends. Why does she have one hand in the air like that?"

"Because she is praying for God to heal her friend. She is holding God's hand until He heals her."

Out of the mouths of babes. I had recently begun praying for my friends for healing and seeing it happen. She knew nothing of this. I had never spoken about it in front of her because I was still figuring it out for myself. Yet here she was, role-playing what was happening spiritually in our home without knowing a single thing about what her mother had been doing.

My son had stopped having nightmares. My daughter was hearing from God in ways I could not explain. God had plans for my husband next.

A week later he told me after evening Bible study that we needed to talk immediately. He was visibly distraught and that made me a little worried. We got home and rushed to tuck the kids in bed. When all was quiet, he sat on the end of our bed and shared that God had convicted him about a secret that he had kept from me. I thought, *This prayer thing really works. Confessions, here we come. . . .*

However, I was not happy to hear what he said next. He reminded me that he had struggled with pornography in high school and some his freshman year in college. I already knew about that, and since it had taken place before we met, it never felt personal. What I did not know was that he did not stop looking at pornography freshman year. Or sophomore. Or the year we got engaged. Or when we got married.

. . . Or in the first few years of our marriage.

I sat frozen.

He shared through tears how he felt out of control at the time and was too ashamed to tell anyone. He told me how he confessed it all to God, who eventually healed him from his addiction. God gave him freedom from pornography and he knew he was forgiven, but now he asked for forgiveness from me.

Would I forgive him for lying all these years? Even though it had taken place over ten years before, it felt fresh. I was hearing the truth for the first time and it stung. Bad.

At first I was passionately angry, clenching my right fist in my left hand as not to hit him. I had never wanted to hit someone before, but for a split second it felt like the appropriate reaction. Then my spiritual armor did what it is supposed to do: It protected me. My choice in the next moment could heal us or break us. God took what the enemy had meant for evil and turned it to good.

In an instant my heart broke for the young man who felt so isolated he had nowhere to turn for help. I released my fist and, instead of hitting him, I wrapped my arms around the man I loved. There is no question in my mind that my hidden prayers had ushered in his confession, and I was proud of him for his courageous vulnerability. I hugged him with all my might and forgave him for keeping that long-hidden secret, praising God for crushing the addiction that could have crushed our marriage.

God had answered every prayer I had prayed for my family—and I had only begun to pray.

What about you? Who and what are you praying for? How do you arm yourself for the battle? Will you be ready for Satan's sneak attacks?

You can be absolutely sure of this truth: "If God is for us, who can be against us?" (Romans 8:31).

Check Your Pulse

1. Do you see the effects of spiritual warfare in your day-to-day life? If so, where? If not, ask God to reveal them to you.

2. How do you prepare yourself for spiritual battle?

3. Of all the pieces of armor, which one do you use the most? Which piece needs to be put on more often?

4. Have you ever prayed over your home? If so, how did it go? If not, what holds you back?

5. Confess any doubts you have had in regard to spiritual warfare or unbelief regarding the power of God to overcome the enemy. How will you learn to walk in His power from now on?

seven

His Presence

The mouthwatering smell of bacon.

You have been there. On a morning off, you have hunkered down in bed for "just five more minutes," when your nostrils are met with the aroma of bacon frying in the pan. Bacon is my nectar from heaven; the cream in my coffee; the reason for getting up in the morning. It comes in a close second to Jesus-y stuff as it lures me out from under the covers with the salty promise of a heart attack in strip form.

I do not hold back come bacon time. Jumping to my feet, I head to the kitchen where a feast awaits. Whether it was when my mother would cook glorious breakfasts for my teenage growth-spurt appetite, or now when my husband spoils me with breakfast on a weekend, the feast is always glorious. The eggs, pancakes stacked high, chilled orange juice, piping hot coffee, yummy syrup—and that too-good-to-be-true bacon. *Pause for applause.*

Heaven will have an all-you-can-eat breakfast buffet, and I am pretty sure it is detailed somewhere in the book of Revelation. ("Let them eat thy bounty in bacon, on earth as it is in heaven.")

Here is where I am headed with this: The presence of the living God is so good that you can almost taste it. Daily, He waits for you with all the best things you could ever imagine, yet most of us let the opportunity to dine with Him slip by. He wants you to spend quality time in His presence, connecting with Him every day. This is when He refreshes your spirit and pours out His love. He has a beautiful table set for you with your name on the best seat, yet you choose to walk by in search of soggy cereal instead. Do you know why? Because cold cereal is the shortcut of breakfasts. Cold. Convenient. Easy.

Even our Christian literature reflects this drive-thru mentality with titles such as *5 Minutes a Day with God, 3 Easy Steps to Transformation, Quick Conversations with the King*, those pre-packaged, easy-to-read guilt-soothers in devotional form. No extra work required. No prep. No extended cleanup. No investment.

But where in the Bible do we ever read about faith being convenient? Why have we neatly packaged our faith to fit into our days, rather than allowing our days to be transformed by our faith?

By failing to make space for Him, we limit Him. A real relationship with God cannot be found through shortcuts. They will never produce the results He intended. Real relationship with Jesus takes skin in the game. It takes sweat and tears. It means dying to self and taking up that cross when it is difficult. If you long for God to change you, throw away your quick-fix, microwave mind-set and embrace the quiet investment of time with Him.

Not a Formula

Our relationship with God does not come with a handbook. There is no guide, only suggestions. A relationship with God is not a mathematical equation where A + B = C every time.

Predictable equations do not require faith, and God understands our human nature well enough to know that when we discover the answer to a problem, we stop asking questions. He loves it when we ask. He did not create us to know all the answers. Knowing it all negates our need for God.

We human beings would trade relationship for rules any day of the week:

> The Lord says: "These people come near to me with their mouth and honor me with their lips, but their hearts are far from me. Their worship of me is based on merely human rules they have been taught."
>
> Isaiah 29:13

All relationships require vulnerability, investment and genuine care. Your marriage cannot be reduced to a to-do list. Your parenting does not consist of Steps One through Five. Any deep, meaningful relationship has ebb and flow, give and take. How two people care for each other in and out of season makes the love real and organic. Robotic love is no love at all.

In comparison to real love, checking off a box is beyond easy. If the rules said "spend time with God," and I did, but I left my heart out of the equation, did I love Him? I always have a choice: to engage on a deeper level or to continue to check off boxes. There is always a third option: God or self. God uses the freedom of choice to cultivate communion with you. He wants you to search and question and discover—and choose Him, over and over.

He says, "You have a question you want answered? Choose to come ask Me. Does a worry weigh on your heart? Choose to share it with Me. Do you struggle to follow Me? Choose to rest in My arms, and I will do the heavy lifting. I am here to save you, but I will not force you to love Me."

In other words, faith is not a formula you choose; it is a freedom you embrace.

What kind of freedom? Freedom from the world's expectations. Freedom from your own sin. Freedom to be yourself before a Father who loves you more than you can fathom. Freedom to follow Him as He gives you His Holy Spirit to show you the way through this sticky life, the Bible to teach you His values and promises and Jesus to bridge the gap from sin to forgiveness. In Him, you and I have all we need to live a new life freely (see 1 Peter 1:3).

Sounds great, right? But what if you do not know how to get to that point? You may be thinking, *How can I know what to do? I need steps to follow or hard-and-fast rules. I never know what He is saying to me or if I am making it up. How can I know for sure that God is the one who is talking to me?*

Please hear me: You are not alone. Every one of us has questioned our ability to hear God. Even seasoned believers get confused. The Bible outlines how we communicate with God and how He communicates with us—in a two-way conversation, not a monologue—and I hope we can break down some of these basic truths. Please keep in mind that these are truths to stand on, not benchmarks by which to measure yourself.

Faith Comes by Hearing

Paul quoted the prophet Isaiah to explain how we come to faith and stay in faith: "Faith comes from hearing the message, and the message is heard through the word about Christ" (Romans 10:16).

The truth is that faith comes by hearing God's message, but how can we be sure that what we are hearing is from Him? We can hear three voices: God's, the enemy's and our own. The sooner we can identify which is which, the easier we can walk in faith, following God's will. It is hard enough to create space in our lives to listen for God's voice, but it can be even harder to sort out whether or not He is speaking. Whose voice is it? Was that God or my own thoughts? Was that me or Satan? How can I know? Let's begin the evaluation process by dissecting the choir of voices in our heads.

"But God doesn't speak to me, Erica." I promise He does. It may not sound the same way to you as it does to me, and that is okay. You may not be able to hear Him clearly yet, but rest assured He has much to say to you. Jesus said as much: "I am the good shepherd; I know my sheep and my sheep know me—just as the Father knows me and I know the Father—and I lay down my life for the sheep" (John 10:14–15). God is your shepherd. His conversations with you are personal because He knows your name. As one of His beloved sheep, you know what His voice sounds like because you listen to it often, and you respond in obedience when you hear it.

In other words, if you are a Christ-follower, then God speaks to you. You are no different than the rest of us. You just need to pay closer attention.

One of the easiest ways to discern God's voice is to measure what you hear against His character. Would a righteous God say what you just heard? How can you find out more about the character of God? Read the Bible. Every book is packed with descriptions of God's character. We read about His love for the unlovable, His gentle redirection, His life-giving words for those who followed Him. When people are troubled, He speaks comforting words, and He asks for submission, not striving. If you want to learn how to recognize God's voice, you must read and even memorize His Word. Then when you think you hear something from Him, you have biblical reference points. Without the Bible, you will never know who God is or what He wants to communicate.

Satan's voice, though, is like "Opposite Day" personified. It will always be the opposite of God's voice. Since God is kind, patient, loving, gracious and gentle, the enemy's voice is mean, impatient, malicious, condemning and harsh. It tells you to work harder, react faster, make your own way and satisfy your own needs. To counter Satan's voice, you must know God's voice—and your own.

I have found that God's voice sounds much like my own, which almost sounds confusing, but I promise it is not. It feels like my own inner voice, although it is always clear and calm. Often when I hear the Holy Spirit speak, it is instant and powerful, like getting struck by lightning (but without the pain). A truth or a prompt may appear as a random thought in my head—*bam*—and I understand it perfectly. However it can take ten minutes to explain the depth of what I heard. God's revelation can be lightning-fast, downloaded immediately. I certainly cannot do something like that in my own power.

God Loves

As I said, God cannot communicate in any way contrary to His character. Therefore, since God is love (see 1 John 4:8), He only speaks to you in a loving way. His love flows throughout the words of the Bible, in both the Old and the New Testaments. For example: "But you are a forgiving God, gracious and compassionate, slow to anger and abounding in love" (Nehemiah 9:17).

That mess-up? He forgives you. When you are mad? He is compassionate. The day you claimed no one loved you? God answered you with His perfect love. When you wrestled with a hard day, God spoke words of love over you; He did not say, "Try harder." He never responds to your sin with the silent treatment. He never pouts until you apologize. His love is inexhaustible.

This does not mean that you will live consequence- or correction-free. God loves you too much to leave you the way you are, and He wants your character to reflect His as you mature in your faith.

Rule of thumb: If the words you hear are loving, that is God's voice.

God Corrects

When you make mistakes (and we all do), God will never ridicule you. He is kind (see Romans 2:4, for example). Therefore you can be sure that any unkind thoughts you have did not come from Him. *You were dumb to try that. You are never going to be good enough.* When you beat yourself up for a mistake or shame yourself for a past sin, God did not send those thoughts. They come from your own heart (often egged on by the enemy's whispered insinuations). God will never bully you or diminish you or poke fun maliciously. Instead, "He guides the humble in what is right and teaches them his way" (Psalm 25:9).

He will not direct you to be unkind toward others, either. Even when another person's sinfulness is obvious and harmful, you will never hear God say something that violates His redeeming love. He would not say, *He's such an idiot* or *There's a lost cause.* You can be sure that your judgmental, unkind or impatient thoughts toward others did not originate in heaven.

God's corrections are gentle and loving. It took me a long time to understand this. I was on edge with God, waiting for Him to bust down the door and yell at me, which He never did. I shrank back from asking Him questions because I was fearful of the punishment I was sure He was waiting to give me. How wrong I was. In reality His corrective words feel like a good friend bringing a word of hope for better, not an enemy condemning you for failure.

If the words you hear restore you and others to a godly life, that is God.

God Promises

The Bible is packed full of God's promises to His people. He takes care of His children, and by that He means you. He has dreams and plans for you:

> His divine power has given us everything we need for a godly life through our knowledge of him who called us by his own glory and goodness. Through these He has given us His very great and precious promises, so that through them you may participate in the divine nature and escape the corruption in the world caused by evil desires.
>
> 2 Peter 1:3–4

His promises are a result of His grace, not our good works. We cannot "earn" God's promises or what He has chosen for us. "Everything we need for a godly life" includes both big and little things. Promises do not have to be grand in scale, only grand in purpose. They will tune your heart toward that which glorifies God, not your own plan. And He will always, always fulfill His promises.

If the words you hear fill you with hope, you can be sure that they come from God.

God Directs

> He makes me lie down in green pastures, he leads me beside quiet waters, he refreshes my soul. He guides me along the right paths for his name's sake.
>
> Psalm 23:2–3

Your word is a lamp for my feet, a light on my path.

Psalm 119:105

God guides and leads you where you need to go. He reveals your path and each step along the way. He directs your work and your rest. The book of Psalms beautifully depicts how God takes time to walk your journey with you, advising you when to move and when to stop. He illuminates which way to go when you come to a fork in the road. He is like a holy Google Maps app, and He is always up to date on the newest roads.

If the words you hear are pointing you toward a path that glorifies Jesus through you, they are God's.

The Enemy's Voice

The enemy speaks in lies. His goals: Condemnation. Guilt. Shame. Pain. His words are ugly. They undermine God's word and refute God's promises. He tells you to keep secrets. He encourages self-promotion and pride. He tells you to take control. He fuels fear and distrust in your heart and mind.

Because his lies are based on truth, though, it can be hard at first to know where the truth leaves off and the lie begins. A prompt from God to treat your body as a temple may twist into obsession about your eating habits. The root of the change in your heart may well be based on truth, while the execution may embody the lie. Satan's words are not backed up with wisdom, and you cannot trace his instruction back to the Bible. What he offers is unsatisfying, destructive, off-color and lust-filled. He tempts you to yield to anger, offense, spite and resentment.

His words are hopeless (*Things will never get better*) or they promise selfish gain (*No one will be better than me*). Satan is a master of disguise, a wolf in sheep's clothing. He will present words and ideas to you that appear good on the surface but that are rotten at the core. We unknowingly follow him to our demise. He has tricked me more than once.

The other day I spoke at a retreat. Speaking from a larger platform is relatively new to me, and I was jazzed for this event. I so wanted it to be my best yet. *God, I want to up my game. I want to be polished and organized so I can honor you with my gift. Please help me nail this one.*

I invested hours in painstaking preparation, writing, tweaking phrases and main points. I reviewed my notes over and over. I begged God to give me success so I would not be a distraction for the women attending. It was then I heard Him speak loud and clear, in the form of a question:

When did you lose your love for my people?

There it was: His easy correction. I knew exactly what He meant. I had made my teaching all about me, and nothing about Him. Somewhere along the way, trying to be my best for God had become more like being the best. *My* ministry, *my* reputation, *my* abilities. I had not spent one minute praying for the women to whom I was ministering. What in the world? This was so uncharacteristic of me.

As I confessed my pride, I felt a weight lift off my shoulders. I had been duped by Satan to focus on myself rather than God, but God did not punish me or rub my nose in my sin. He presented a question to bring my heart back into alignment with Him. The Holy Spirit revealed my heart instantly. I confessed this all later to my close friend who confirmed what I had heard by sharing a powerful Scripture:

> Therefore, since through God's mercy we have this ministry, we do not lose heart. Rather, we have renounced secret and shameful ways; we do not use deception, nor do we distort

the word of God. . . . For what we preach is not ourselves, but Jesus Christ as Lord, and ourselves as your servants for Jesus' sake.

2 Corinthians 4:1–2, 5

The enemy had presented me with a partial truth, "Whatever you do, work at it with all your heart" (Colossians 3:23) but slipped in the idea that I should make it happen on my own, apart from God. Oops. I forgot that doing anything without love is fruitless and noisy (see 1 Corinthians 13). Half-truths and twisted words are Satan's specialty. This is why knowing God's Word is essential and staying in constant communion with Him is nonnegotiable.

In summary, if the words you hear (i.e., the thoughts you think) contradict God's Word, call and character in any way, they originate with the enemy.

My Voice

My own voice can be very quick to recommend whatever will make me most comfortable or will elevate me above God. My voice will affirm all things cozy and easy, steer me away from fear, and highlight how awesome I am.

The easiest way to distinguish between my voice and the Holy Spirit is to test the direction I feel God may be leading. How does it make me feel? How does my spirit react? If I imagine myself following through with what the voice said, would the result glorify God?

You cannot hold back because of a natural fear, nor do you want to jump blindly into an unwise choice. Do a heart check: What are your motives? How will you achieve them? Is this a gut feeling that will not go away?

If you can answer these questions with a pure heart, then take a baby step. Start working toward that which you believe may be God's calling. If it ends up that your own mind was doing the talking, that is okay. Repent and try it God's way. When He corrected me for following my own agenda for that retreat teaching, I did it His way instead of running away from the assignment. Can I tell you it was the most powerful teaching I have ever delivered? Because it was all about Him, I saw Him work in a breathtaking way.

God will not hold it against you when you sincerely mess it up. It is a process of trial and error. The more conversations you have with God, the better you will know His voice (and your own). The more time you spend in His presence, the less you will question His calling. The more you allow Him to refine and mature you, the less of your sinful nature will clog lines of communication when you call on Him.

Your Voice Is Not Always Bad

I knew God had big plans.

God and I were going on a date, just the two of us. No kids, no husband, no rules. Given the option of any activity under the sun, my mind went into hyperdrive. Oh, the possibilities: I could read! I could write! I might even take a nap if time permitted. The sky was the limit. My open-ended opportunity offered abundant promise and rest, but I could not take even my first step. All that freedom was strangling me. My brain was over-processing what I was "supposed" to do.

There were those invisible rules again.

Do I jump straight to the have-to's, so I don't waste my time? Should I be adventurous and go on a hike? Would it be helpful to bring my Bible? Should I journal or not? Write or not write? Perfectionism is exhausting.

God had been showing me something: As He has been molding me, He has refined my desires. He has proven that my natural inclination is not always bad. Quite often, as I have learned to reject anything that is not of God, I have embraced His voice as my own. When I hear or see what I should do next, I can be thinking thoughts from the Holy Spirit, not only those of my own mind. I replaced my old self-denial method of hearing God with my motto for the day: "Be yourself."

Instead of shutting down my personality, free will and natural bent, I decided to embrace it, just to see what would happen. This new concept felt fresh and amazingly like, well, me. To determine what I would do for my date, I asked myself, "What would Erica like to do?" Erica would love to get a cup of coffee to start her special date. Yes! That sounded right. I would do whatever Erica would naturally do, and trust that God would guide my steps.

I had already picked the perfect place to encounter God—a small town that still preserves its past in a beautiful way. The old county square is adorable, reminiscent of days gone by. The tiny shops look like dominoes, stacked upright like cramped children on a school bus, each one competing for the front. Flags hang from the old-timey awnings and sandwich board signs announce the daily specials.

I sought a familiar coffee shop, determined to be Me while finding God. The space inside was somewhat empty, but the atmosphere was cheerful. I ordered my usual and stood at the counter to wait. The barista was eager to chat, a common characteristic of Texans. She asked me how my day was, to which I would normally reply, "Great. Yours?" but today I felt a voice prompting me to explain why I was there.

"It's a good day; I am on a writing retreat."

"That's so cool! Have you ever been to the nature sanctuary? You have to go. It has trails and butterfly houses. It's great.

People from out of town don't usually know about it, but I love to go!"

Of course.

I should not have been surprised that she would tell me about a place I had never heard of that would be perfect for a day of seclusion and reflection, in the middle of nature, the very thing Erica adores. I had been praying God would show me "what, when and where" for my time with Him, and He gave me an exact address. I found it by being Me, doing what Me does. I did not mess up the plan.

When I am looking to encounter God's presence, a deep truth presents itself: If I am submitted to the process, God is committed to my progress.

In other words, I cannot mess it up. I am not powerful enough to thwart the plans and purposes of God. If my heart is leaning in to hear Him and my feet are inclined to follow Him, He will guide me. Absolutely. I used to believe that to be more like God and to hear every word He had for me, I would need to repress all of who I was. But when I surrender myself to God, I am allowing Him to do what He does best: make His name famous. There is no need to erase who I am in order to follow God obediently. The two go hand in hand. As He refines me, I become more like Him. The more I surrender, the more my identity reflects Jesus.

My submission + His presence = A safe place to be

I do not need to follow a confusing formula or recite special words. I simply need to spend time with God. My busy-ness makes it even more essential to carve out time for this relationship. I cannot compose a timeline for the time we spend together. There is no schedule. He is in charge and I am not.

All I can bring is my flaws. All I can ask Him is to show up in spite of them. He never required perfection—I did. I was scared to bring my true self, with all its flaws and sins, before

Him and let Him examine me. I was afraid He would punish me or ridicule me for my mistakes. Instead He healed me.

Check Your Pulse

1. Do you hear God speak to you on a regular basis? What does His voice sound like to you?
2. Name some truths God has spoken about you. If you have never asked, take time to ask Him now. God has sweet words to speak to you.
3. Describe a time you heard God, without question. How did it feel? What did He say? What did you see?
4. There may be lies you believe about the voice of God. Ask the Holy Spirit to reveal those to you right now.
5. If you have ever claimed, "God doesn't speak to me," confess that right now. Repent for speaking a lie over yourself and ask God to break down any walls that are keeping you from hearing Him.

eight

Shedding Skin

"I knew God was talking to me through the butterflies." The woman stood at the front of the room with a beatific smile on her face.

I almost gagged. Her testimony of God's love was about fluttering butterflies? That worn-out old analogy? *Puhleeze . . .* "Transformation . . ." "Beautiful creature that once crawled in the dirt."

While I quietly respected her time to share, my insides were crying out, *Unacceptable. Somebody tell her how silly she sounds.* My mocking heart sputtered with outrage.

Then God's Spirit pulled me up short. I remembered what Jesus once said (see Matthew 5:28) about the intentions of our hearts being just as important as our outer behavior, and how if I harbor hate or dislike in my heart and I fail to check it, I am sinning just as if I had given public expression to it.

Everything flows out from our hearts, good and bad. No quick fix or Band-Aid will correct a sinful heart; God must replace it completely. It is a process of surrender—the old must die and the new must come to life. The redemption of Christ moves from dark to light, death to life, like a caterpillar becoming a butterfly.

Caterpillar to butterfly? Oh, man. The butterfly illustration is perfect after all. I stand corrected.

We cannot stay the same forever if we are going to become a new creation, remade in the image of our Creator. We must learn and grow and release and change, letting the weight of our old self be stripped away. Some of that weight may have been placed on us by others, and it becomes heavier because of the shame and guilt we choose to carry. It is like old, dead skin that we must shed in order to allow the new to grow.

This brings to mind what happened when a friend of mine decided she needed a facial chemical peel. This procedure removes the top layers of skin through a chemical applied to the skin, causing it to exfoliate and eventually peel off, taking with it the damaged skin and revealing the younger skin underneath. It is meant to take years off one's complexion. My friend wanted her baby face to be restored, and in order to do so she was willing to go through a tremendous amount of pain. She came to a family event a few days after her treatment and I grimaced when I saw her skin. Looking at her face hurt my face.

"What happened?" I asked her, shocked at the results.

"Oh, this is what happens when you remove the top layer of your skin. It is really painful and I hate it, but I know it will be worth it."

She was too optimistic for my taste. Had she looked in the mirror? She had *paid* someone to inflict that pain? It seemed like a form of torture. Please slap some sense into me if I decide to use the same fountain-of-youth cheese grater on my face. Count me out, amiga.

While I may run from pain and discomfort, I do not want to run from the kind of pain that is necessary for personal growth. Am I willing to go through the pain of shedding my own skin—er, *sin*? We all have dead layers of sin that need to be peeled off and thrown away. Under all those layers of hurt and disappointment we will find grace and hope. We will never embrace that new person if first we do not endure the painful process of transformation. We will never be made new until the old layers are taken away.

I used to be famous for using the "That's what she said," tagline. I could always get a laugh. Then the voice of God convicted me: *Not cool, Erica. Not cool.* Sure, I knew it was a little risqué, but nothing harmful. It definitely carried sexual overtones and some jokes might be made in poor taste (but those are some of the best). I wrestled and wrestled with letting go of that stupid phrase until God asked me, *Why is this so hard to let go? Why do you hold it so tightly?*

I was stumped. Why should I care so deeply about continuing to use that particular phrase? You would think it would be easy to let go of, but it proved to be a difficult step of obedience. God and I began a dialogue that ultimately led to my confession. Aloud I spoke the phrase, "I am proud that I can hang with the guys, okay?"

I had cultivated a personality that was deeply sarcastic and a little off-color, not overly offensive, but enough to blend in. Guys felt comfortable to be themselves around me and I was proud of that. I was proud I could hold my own backstage with the guys in the band. I was proud when they apologized for saying something inappropriate in my hearing and I could say, "Oh it's fine. I'm not like other girls. It doesn't bother me," and mean it. "That's what she said" was my gateway drug into pride and proving myself, both of which are sin.

God began to show me that such jokes *should* bother me. I found where Paul wrote about it:

> Do not let any unwholesome talk come out of your mouths, but only what is helpful for building others up according to their needs, that it may benefit those who listen. . . . Nor should there be obscenity, foolish talk or coarse joking, which are out of place, but rather thanksgiving.
>
> Ephesians 4:29; 5:4

My words should be uplifting. With the Holy Spirit living in me, my reactions should be different. If my guy friends apologized for their language or behavior, I should accept their apology. This was a new way of looking at everything: to think that if my words and actions do not agree with my God, then they should not agree with me. I had stood firmly on that piece of my identity for long enough. It was time to let God reshape the words I spoke.

I determined to clean up my potty mouth by sheer force. I heard every excuse in my head. *It's not even like you are cussing. This is stupid. You should be able to say what you want. You are such a good person and you also say such sweet things to people. You should have this one outlet.* Oh, the lies we hear.

When my will alone could not shape my transformation successfully, I tried a new method. Instead of trying harder to curb my words, I released my grip on them. My words were no longer mine. Not one. When someone set me up for the perfect "That's what she said" line, I released it to God instead of saying it. Every word was now submitted before it left my mouth. Difficult? Yes. Impossible? Not in the slightest.

Shedding the skin of one's identity can be insanely difficult if we hold it too tightly. But what a glorious exchange, our old for His new, when we let go. When we release our grip, we are free to grab hold of what else God has for us.

When we accept Jesus, God gives us a new heart. Brand spankin' new! In the words of the prophet Ezekiel: "I will give them an undivided heart and put a new spirit in them; I will remove from them their heart of stone and give them a heart of flesh" (Ezekiel 11:19). God is the perfect heart surgeon, not only removing the old, sick heart, but also replacing it with a better one. He can trace each vein and artery. He knows which ones are blocked and which are healthy and strong. He can open up that chest cavity and clean everything up, making it as beautiful as it was created to be.

When God pointed out that seemingly insignificant phrase to me, it was His way of beginning to assess my heart damage. My need to hang with the guys stemmed from years of falsely believing that girls were horrible and boys were awesome. "Boys rule and girls drool," I recited, even though I happened to be female. "That's what she said" was a symptom of my sickness; it traced back to my heart of stone. Unless I eliminated that phrase, my heart would never be healthy.

Anyone who undergoes heart surgery comes home from the hospital with a very long list of foods that are off-limits if they want to keep their heart in tip-top shape. What about our spiritual hearts? What does God prescribe and forbid?

God's list did not stop with cleaning up my speech. Oh no, that would be too easy. He threw in the TV shows I watched. There were some fantastic shows that I loved dearly. The writing was superb and the casts were outstanding. Why can I not watch those, God? I guess they did glorify acts that God is not cool with—murder, bad language, the random sex scene. In fact, nothing I watched was wholesome or uplifting. Those shows may have been funny or suspenseful, but they were not healthy choices for my new heart.

Television was like the greasy cheeseburger of my heart, and I am speaking as someone for whom greasy burgers are still my jam. No matter how I craved that artisanal bun soaked in creamy cheese and butter, I knew it would put me right back in the doctor's office. I cut out those shows completely.

Does that mean I could never eat "meat"? No. But I needed to make sure the meat I ingested from then on was good. Rather than a greasy cheeseburger, I needed to choose a lean patty wrapped in lettuce. Television is not all bad; the shows I chose to watch were. I could sit down and watch television, but when the show contained aspects that would hurt my new heart, I turned them off. The healthier my heart grew, the better my filter was for what to take in and not take in. Music, books, even conversations I had with friends were under the scrutiny of my Dietician. *Erica, do you need that? How will it make you feel later? Later tonight when you cannot sleep, will you regret it?*

You know what? With my heart cleaned from those bad habits, I could hear God more clearly than ever before.

Jesus spoke only the words God told him to speak. (See John 14:10.) He stripped out the language He may have wanted to use—offhand remarks, dividing opinions, jokes—all thrown aside for the sake of the One He represented. We must do the same. It is time to throw off whatever hinders us so we can run the race God has set before us:

> Let us throw off everything that hinders and the sin that so easily entangles. And let us run with perseverance the race marked out for us, fixing our eyes on Jesus, the pioneer and perfecter of faith.
>
> Hebrews 12:1–2

Losing Weight

My dad has always been my hero. Some of my fondest memories of him are from my elementary school days, when he would exit the bathroom after getting ready for the office and I would breathe in the strong, musky smell of Drakkar Noir. He stood tall and lean at 6 feet 2 inches, but his level of confidence made him seem a foot taller. His German blond hair combed and perfectly styled, crisp white polo shirt tucked into his braided leather belt and cool set of aviator sunglasses shielding his eyes, he always looked down and smiled at me as he climbed into his Bronco and waved good-bye each morning. I am still convinced nobody else was ever more comfortable in his own skin.

But we all change as we age, gaining wrinkles and weight we never anticipated, and my dad was no different. The increase in the number on his bathroom scale never lowered my opinion of him, but it began to plague his own self-worth. Finally fed up with the extra weight he was carrying around, he committed to lose the pounds. Because he is an all-or-nothin' kind of guy he enlisted the help of doctors to closely monitor his weight loss. My dad has never met a goal he could not conquer, and his weight was about to go down.

In less than 6 months, my dad lost 65 pounds. 65! That did not happen because he crossed his fingers and made wishes for the fat to melt away. It took discipline and hard work. He recognized where he needed to change and he worked hard to achieve it.

Whether it is losing weight or becoming a more faithful Christian, you must play a part in the upkeep of your own transformation. Change is an ever-growing process of choosing discipline over decadence.

God replaces our heart of stone with a heart of flesh; this is certain. But somewhere along the way we must introduce self-control. God can work miracle after miracle for you, but if you keep returning to drink the poison, He cannot set you free. You have a choice to follow His prescription for your new heart. He will not force you to change.

One of the fruits of the Spirit is self-control. (See Galatians 5:22–23.) This means that I have been given power from God to manage the thoughts, emotions and intent of my own body and mind. I am not a victim of my life, I am a victor. More of God means more self-control. More self-control means a healthier heart. A healthier heart means more space for God to communicate with me. Out with the old and in with the new.

Do you ever feel like your brain is filled with continuous thoughts? Checklists, schedules, songs, television shows and even lies we believe develop into constant chatter in our minds. Keeping track of all of that chatter leaves no space for God to speak. Once I stopped watching so much television, I no longer craved TV. In the moments when I had some quiet time to myself (which were not many), I was no longer subconsciously replaying a show in my mind. I was no longer singing song lyrics that were nasty or contradictory to what I believed. I was now hearing God's voice instead. When I let my mind wander, I could now hear the voice of God loud and clear. Why? Because I had lost the weight of my sin and I had room for Him.

Let me tell you—hearing that voice is addicting! Knowing what was coming up in my day or how to handle a stressful situation filled me more than any show or song ever could. That quiet space gave me insight into God's will like never before. It did not require a long, legalistic process to "get my heart right" and hear from God. It was now instant conversation, the most gratifying Q and A I have ever experienced. By laying down my wants in favor of His, in turn I wanted more of what He had to give.

Dropping weight takes both discipline and time. My dad did not drop 65 pounds overnight, and you will not hear God with absolute clarity right away, either. You have to cut the junk—for good—and it may take a while to show results. Dad's diet was closely monitored. If he cheated on his diet, he did not let it derail him. He picked himself up and got in line with what he knew he needed to do. He began to run daily. He got stronger and faster the more he trained. We ran a half-marathon together to celebrate his transformation.

In our spiritual lives, failure recognized and reprogrammed is solid evidence of our heart transplant.

What do you need to do? Where are you carrying extra weight spiritually? How are you exercising self-control to make space for God? For me it was my humor and my media consumption, but it has not stopped there. It continues to grow as He asks me more questions. How I love others. How I raise my kids. The kind of wife I am. There is room to grow in all areas of my life.

Each time I "work out" spiritually, I am training my mental, spiritual and emotional muscles to grow into the shape that God desires—but I need to remember that no one will do it for me. I have to show up at the gym. I have to lace up my shoes. I have to say no to dessert. I have to keep showing up, even on the days when I want to quit, not because I have to, but because I want to.

The results of a clean heart outweigh the benefits of an entertained mind. It is not legalism when we are sincere. We do not cut out everything and become hermits who cannot function in society. We let the Spirit guide us, filtering every decision through Him.

The Opinions of Others

I know what you are thinking. *I don't want to be the weird kid.*

No one wants to feel like an outsider. When the talk around the office is about last night's episode of fill-in-the-blank, you will not have any thoughts to contribute. No opinions about which housewife backstabbed the other housewife. You will be at a loss when everyone is providing their guess as to who killed whom in the latest mature-rated show. When they ask why you do not watch these shows, what will your answer be? If you say, "Because God has better for me," they may ridicule you or even persecute you. Or ignore you and isolate you.

They can do all this and worse, but it will be worth it. They do not understand God's call on your life. Unless they themselves are seeking God (and sometimes even then), they cannot wrap their brains around why you are sacrificing what you do.

You are not alone. Scripture tells us:

> If you are insulted because of the name of Christ, you are blessed, for the Spirit of glory and of God rests on you. If you suffer, it should not be as a murderer or thief or any other kind of criminal, or even as a meddler. However, if you suffer as a Christian, do not be ashamed, but praise God that you bear that name.
>
> 1 Peter 4:14–16

It hurts to be judged for your faith. No one wants to face ridicule for following Jesus, but it is inevitable. Your response when it happens is crucial to your testimony. If you lash out or try to prove that your way is the best way, you will miss the point. Your uniqueness in your workplace or neighborhood is a blessing. You are bearing the brunt of their insults, yet it is for an amazing reason: You are being remade in the image of Christ. If He was persecuted, you will be also. What a beautiful gift.

As you continue to grow, God will continue to set you apart. A loving father will not let his children continue in foolishness. He corrects and guides them to a better way. God will keep pouring into you as long as you respond to His refining hand.

A friend once told me she asked God what outfit to wear each day. I distinctly remember thinking, *She must be weird. And exhausted.* I had no interest in being either. *Pray about my clothes? That's taking things a little far, don't you think?* I did not want to be strange. I wanted to be a cool Christian, the one who talks about God only at the most un-awkward times and who never uses "Christianese."

These days, however, I ask God what to wear each day. Did you know He has an opinion about that? He cares about every detail.

As I shed layer after layer of old skin, I quickly found out that God wants me to share more with others. I have shared words with people when God told me to, even when the words sounded cheesy and uncool. I have given away the shoes I was wearing, the jacket off my back, jewelry that I cherished—all to show someone else the love of God. With the layers of lies and worry gone from my heart, I no longer cared what others thought about my walk with God. That was my business, not theirs. My calling was to care about God's opinion and no one else's.

Do you want that kind of heart, free from fear and expectation? God has words He longs to whisper in your ear, but up to now you have not been able to hear Him because you have not let go. He wants to set you free from caring about others' opinions, but your grip on pleasing others is too tight. His hand is outstretched to lift you out of your circumstances, but you refuse to be disciplined enough to stay out. Today, you have a choice: keep doing the same ol' same ol', or trade in this old tired life for a new one.

Welcome the change God has for you. He is a loving God who cannot wait to walk with you into the next phase of your faith.

Check Your Pulse

1. Do you have a fear of change? Why or why not?
2. Have you ever sacrificed a part of your past that hurt to let go of? What was it? How did God work in your life once you let go?

3. What part of your heart has God restored for Himself? Are you guarding your new heart through self-control?

4. Describe a time you felt embarrassed by your faith. Have you ever received God's acceptance at a time when others did not accept you?

5. List the habits and strongholds that God wants you to surrender to Him. Pray for the strength to follow Him fully in these areas.

nine

Good-bye Fear

Joey is a true Texan. Being born and raised under the Texas flag bred a self-confidence that most people envy. Whether this is a good or bad thing, time will tell.

From what I hear about his growing-up years, his superconfidence led Joey and his friends into a number of ventures that were outstandingly risky and downright dumb. I have often wondered, "Joey. How are you still alive?"

One of his favorite places to get into trouble was a lake called "P.K." I did not find out till years later that this stood for "Possum Kingdom."

There must have been a shortage of good lake names that year.

He and his friends would take a ski boat out into the massive lake and spend the day tubing and water skiing. One day someone got the bright idea that they should jump off The Cliffs. Yes, that is capitalized for a reason. The Cliffs are no small hill on the edge of the lake. We are talking about a rock ledge sixty feet off the water. The lip of the rock juts out just enough so that, if you are lucky, you can jump out far enough to miss the rocks just below the water's surface. Who would not want to jump off that?

There is dumb luck and just plain dumb, and jumping off The Cliffs was the latter. Joey and his friends did it. He says he would do it again even today, but since he wishes to stay married to me, he refrains.

When God challenges us to refine our faith, we may feel we are jumping off a cliff. Unlike Joey and his friends, we hesitate to follow through. The great thing about God is He does not ask us to do anything foolish. Jumping from His cliff is not a death-defying feat, but rather a step toward growing our faith. After we jump once, the fear subsides and we are ready for bigger heights.

Sharing your faith with another may feel terrifying, but after you do it once you gain confidence and deeper trust in God. While choosing to jump from The Cliffs at P.K. was a risk, trusting God is never a gamble.

Every time we jump for the sake of following God, our feet will find His solid foundation. The Christian bubble some of us live in feels safe. Church, private Christian schools, Christian book clubs and mom groups. Everyone involved has the same moral standards and world view. Conversely, having faith in the "real," or secular, world may feel like the scariest thing we have ever faced. Thankfully we have some pretty great people in the Bible who showed us how to do it well. Paul is one of them. Paul knew that trusting God was always his best option, even when he was most afraid. He never gave up. He was too legit to quit.

The Sinking Ship

In Acts 27 we read the story of Paul, who was a prisoner traveling by sea under guard, and how his faith played out in the midst of seeming disaster.

You have to wonder why the sailors and guards who had been charged with the transport of the prisoners set sail in the first place. They had reached the end of the season for sailing. Their odds of a trip going well were iffy at best. By heading out when they did, they faced extreme storms and possible death, but hey, what would life be without a little impending doom? They chose to take the risk.

Have you ever felt like the people in charge of big decisions that affect your life maybe should not be in charge? Paul understands your pain. He tried to talk the headstrong men out of their plan, but they were called headstrong for a reason and refused to relent. They loaded on board the prisoners, the supplies and an ample amount of bravado, and embarked on their voyage.

Like a Hollywood movie, the suspense builds. The worst-case scenario is coming to pass: A violent storm stirs up and it is going down for real. The Bible account sums it up: "When neither sun nor stars appeared for many days and the storm continued raging, we finally gave up all hope of being saved" (Acts 27:20).

Yep. That sounds about right. Talk about a low point.

If you were Paul, how would you react? All signs point to "dead" on the survival radar and you are chained to the dude next to you. No lifejacket. No life at all if you are on that boat much longer. I am pretty sure I would have peed my pants by then, at least a little bit. For certain I would have thrown up. More than likely I would be on my knees on the farthest corner of the ship, praying for God to take me quickly, in Jesus' name.

Paul, however, is a shining example of a Jesus Freak. Instead of freaking out, he keeps his head—and then some. As the ship is thrashing back and forth, he gives the men on the ship a little pep talk:

I urge you to keep up your courage, because not one of you will be lost; only the ship will be destroyed. Last night an angel of the God to whom I belong and whom I serve stood beside me and said, "Do not be afraid, Paul. You must stand trial before Caesar; and God has graciously given you the lives of all who sail with you." So keep up your courage, men, for I have faith in God that it will happen just as he told me.

Acts 27:22–25

Talk about confidence. Let's glean from Paul's courage. Notice the story does not say, "The storm calmed for a moment so Paul could gather the men together for a nice chat in the sun." Paul is in the middle of a storm that God has confirmed is going to destroy the ship. This was no fly-by rain shower. It was a horrific sight; the waves were starting to splinter the sides of the ship into obliteration.

Yet here is Paul, hardly able to keep his footing as the waves crash and the wind howls, declaring, "God says we are cool, guys, totally safe. I mean, the ship will be nonexistent when we reach the shore, but we cool."

Then he just has to add, "P.S. You are *sooo* lucky. God would have let you die here on this ship, but because He really likes me, He is going to spare you. It is a good thing He likes me. You're welcome."

I can see the men's eyes piercing Paul like daggers. If Paul is anything, it is unapologetic about repeating what God says to him. I like that. #nofilter

The drama continues. The storm does not end after that speech. It grows in intensity. The men are now facing day fourteen of this madness. This is the hurricane that never ends. Then it gets worse. The men cannot take it anymore, and who can blame them? The sailors begin to sense they are coming up on land, but they are unable to see two feet in front of the ship.

They are terrified they will be dashed against the rocks of the shore and die. In desperation they drop their anchors, hoping to catch something solid that could save their lives, praying for daylight to come quickly.

Seems like a decent strategy to me. But just then, two geniuses ruin it all with their brilliant plan to save their own lives, never mind everyone else. They plan to secretly lower the lifeboat into the water and get away to safety while they still can.

Here is the problem with their plan: In order for everyone on the ship to survive, they needed to keep all hands on deck to man the boat. Their sneaking away would guarantee certain death for the others. Paul, being the self-assured guy that he is, sees what is happening and cuts the rope to the lifeboat. Splash goes the boat.

Paul was not good at making friends.

Just before the sun rises, Paul delivers a great speech for the desperate men. He acknowledges their fear, tells them to eat something (because who can be brave on an empty stomach?) and reminds them of God's promise that they will not die. Paul is not afraid to react differently because he knows trusting God is a sure thing. Uncommon boldness in fearful circumstances is a hallmark of Paul.

He then stands up, thanks God for the bread he is about to eat, and chows down. I love how the men respond. The pep talk worked. According to the account: "They were all encouraged and ate some food themselves" (Acts 27:36).

Sometimes, when we are scared, we shut down the bold faith we are given by God. We allow mistrust in God's plan to govern our heart when we are fearful. It does not have to be this way. When fear sets in and we cannot take the next step into the stormy deep, when graduating to the next level in our faith scares us, we can stand firm in the comfort He provides. Paul's faith was consistently being pushed beyond the norm. He kept throwing away everything for the sake of following Jesus. Forget arm floaties—he dove into the deep end, head first. Because He trusted the God who beckoned him to deeper waters, he could see the promise that would be fulfilled if he stepped out in faith.

When the Going Gets Tough

What can we learn from Paul's faith under these extreme circumstances? Let's look back at the story.

We must trust that God will provide for our needs.

We know that Paul had a good night's sleep. While all the other men on the boat were sleepless with terror, Paul was not afraid. I have a hard time falling asleep with an extra-long to-do list in my brain, let alone snoozing while a life-threatening storm is rocking the very bed in which I sleep. But just think about it: Paul's sleep was so deep that he had a dream in which an angel appeared and called him by name. Only by God's grace was Paul able to sleep on that ship. God knew he would need all his energy to follow through with the huge tasks ahead, including facing Caesar, so He provided sweet sleep.

When we follow God into deeper water, He reveals His plan.

Paul's dream was powerful. The angel showed Paul the purpose of his current situation and what effect his call had on others. Meeting Caesar face-to-face was part of God's big plan for his life. Because of Paul's willingness to risk everything, God's favor is pouring all over Paul, saturating him and splashing onto the other men on the ship.

Compared to how we often feel—alone, sans purpose and significance—Paul had it easy. He got a message straight from an angel. What could be more supernatural and clear than that? God was moving Paul to preach in a new location and he was promised safety—but not smooth sailing. Paul was right where he needed to be to experience more of God: in the midst of a storm. God always has more for us when He is growing our trust in His plan—more revelation, more challenge, more growth and in Paul's case, even an angel.

God loves us deeply.

Notice the language used by Paul to remind the men of God's promise of safety: "Not one of you will lose a single hair from his head" (Acts 27:34).

This statement shows an impressive familiarity of the words of Jesus, because it reflects Jesus' statement that we find in the books of Luke and Matthew:

> Are not two sparrows sold for a penny? Yet not one of them will fall to the ground outside your Father's care. And even the very hairs of your head are all numbered. So don't be afraid; you are worth more than many sparrows.
>
> Matthew 10:29–31

> Indeed the very hairs of your head are all numbered. Don't be afraid; you are worth more than many sparrows.
>
> Luke 12:7

Each and every person is valuable in the eyes of God. If God cares for the tiny sparrows, who are not made in His image, how much more will He keep and care for us? If we are held in the protective hand of God, what can hurt us beyond physical death? There is no harm inflicted that heaven cannot heal.

Paul is reminding the men on this sinking ship of the vastness of God's love for them. He has numbered the hairs on each of their heads and evidently this was not the time for them to lose any. (Hey, fellas, not only will God save you from death by shipwreck, He has not signed you up as poster children for Rogaine any time soon, either.)

God, in His loving grace, provided courage when it was most needed. He brought hope in the form of a man named Paul, who spoke the words of Christ. Though Paul was a prisoner, he was truly the freest man on the ship.

When we are fearful, God is faithful.

The men on the ship became so scared they were desperate for safety. The situation was out of their control: exhaustion, hunger, dark waves crashing against the bow, no sense of direction. It made them crazy. They needed somebody to speak with a voice of reason and to show them what to do.

Thanks, Paul, for being the designated driver.

In Acts 27:33, Paul states the obvious: "It has been fourteen days of craziness. You guys have not been eating. You're a little hangry. Grab a Snickers and regroup, because y'all are actin' a fool" (paraphrase by Erica Willis).

These men listened to Paul because they knew they could trust him, and we must listen to the Holy Spirit when He calls to us in the midst of difficulties. When we are reluctant to trust because of fear, we must recognize our fear, call it what it is and replace it with God's truth.

Later Paul summed it up in his advice to Timothy: "For the Spirit God gave us does not make us timid [fearful], but gives us power, love and self-discipline" (2 Timothy 1:7).

God is greater than our fear. Fear should have no hold over any of us. It should never keep us from the goodness that God has for us. But if we do not see that we are being influenced by fear, then we cannot conquer it. Paul was cool as a cucumber. That was all it took: naming fear, a reminder of God's power and intentional trust.

Trusting God gives Him permission to work however He desires. It takes us out of our limitations and places us into His limitlessness.

We need to thank God in the middle of our storm.

Paul was breaking bread and thanking God while sitting on a sinking ship. This was far from comfortable. But it could never have happened if they had enjoyed a perfect voyage.

Perfect scenarios blind us to the hand of God because we mistakenly feel that we did it all, that somehow our own abilities and gifts conjured up the dream world we are living in. However, when we find ourselves on our faces before God, begging for His intervention, we remember how small and powerless we truly are. The heavy weight of tragedy and disappointment brings to light our inadequacies—thereby highlighting God's bigness. In those times, we can sing His praises from the bottom of our hearts, for without Him we have nothing. We recognize God for who He is and for what He does. As a result, we begin to dream again, believing that even miracles are possible. Our hope is restored.

By breaking bread and giving thanks, Paul pointed every man on that ship back to the Creator of the sea, who cared about them and who deserved thanks and praise.

We go all in.

After fourteen days of terror, the men finally relaxed enough to eat. Once they had their fill of bread, they threw the rest of the grain overboard and committed themselves to God's providence. In essence, they recognized their sin, trusted God to care for them and rested in His promise that they would survive. It is the same with us. Once we seek God, we no longer have to strive for solutions. No more strategizing and manipulating to get ahead. He just shows us what to do and how to do it.

When did you last have an opportunity to trust God like this? Were you fearful? He did not drag you into deeper waters kicking and screaming, did He? He simply offered His hand as He led you to a depth that requires more faith in Him than the shallow end does. He will never shove you into the ocean and walk away. He loves you too much to do that. You do not have to take care of yourself.

Are you willing to throw all of your bread overboard?

Our Faith in the Real World

Standing for truth and God in a world that rejects both is neither easy nor fun. This faith He calls us to live out can feel like a curse, in the worst way. Why must we be so often rejected? Why must our hearts long for a home so far from where we are? Why will others not open their ears to our message?

We have not been made for this world. We are aliens among natives, trapped temporarily in a sort of limbo between restoration and completion. Though heaven is our home, earth is where we get our mail. Since we will remain here until He takes us home, we must learn to function in the friction. In other words: "We are hard pressed on every side, but not crushed; perplexed, but not in despair; persecuted, but not abandoned; struck down but not destroyed" (2 Corinthians 4:8–9).

Living out our faith is difficult but it cannot steal our joy. The real world comes knocking to rob us of all that is good and holy about our communion with God, but we refuse to answer the door. We remain strong and firm. When the world around us shivers in the storm, we stand on the deck and declare His deeds. We eat among the sinners and the broken because they need Jesus the way we need Jesus. Dying to ourselves, we face our fears head on and come out stronger for it.

This world is not your home. This world will chew you up and spit you out. This world is like shifting shadows, casting doubt over anything it touches.

Who Are You?

Maybe your story is like Paul's—one of strength and faith in the face of an ocean of unknown.

Maybe you are less like Paul and more like the very scared (read "cautious") men on the ship. You are desperate for God to save you from the waters that terrify you. You believe that going deeper with God will certainly feel like drowning, and no one wants to feel that, especially you.

I have been both types, depending on the situation. My boldness takes center stage when I know in my heart of hearts that God has talked to me. Other times I shrink back in self-doubt and worry, avoiding the next step into the depths. *How will I keep my head above water? Will anyone save me if I start to sink? I cannot do this alone. I am not a strong swimmer.* Maybe you cannot swim either, and that is actually okay. God wants to teach us how to swim, but we must put our trust in Him.

You would not be the first to confuse "learning to swim" with "drowning," and you will not be the last. Everyone faces fear. You know what? God does not hold your lack of faith against you. Instead He offers you courage to face your enemies, truth when you hear only lies, food when the hunger becomes overwhelming and clarity in the chaos.

Letting the Holy Spirit begin to guide and shape your path requires faith. Without faith, you can do nothing.

Fear makes us switch into fight-or-flight mode. Fighting, we scramble to make a way for ourselves. We kick and bite whatever scares us until we win or they run away. Or we turn tail and run away from our adversary. This is how our bodies were created to react to fear. But God offers a third option: love.

What if, instead of running or fighting, you let God replace your fear with love? At last, you could shift out of survival mode. No longer would you have to work so hard to keep your head above water. You could swim without growing weary. You could jump off that stupid-high cliff and not break one bone. God's love shatters the strongholds that keep us chained in this world. Following the hand of God leads us deeper, and His love drives our fear away. His touch on us enables us to be brave and try new steps of faith.

He will give you exactly what you need. Honor Him. Trust Him. He will take you all the way to the other shore. Are you ready to enter deeper waters?

Check Your Pulse

1. Name a fear that you faced and conquered. How did you do it? How did that make you feel?

2. How have you been scared to live out your faith in front of others? What have you learned about yourself that will help you become bolder?

3. Identify a fear you face. What verses in the Bible speak directly to your fear, and how can you personally utilize these to retrain your mind and heart to trust God?

4. Paul inspires me to stay faithful when my world is falling apart. What part of the shipwreck story inspires you most?

5. The storm Paul endured led to preaching the message of Christ to new people groups. What bigger plan may God have in allowing you to endure your current storm?

PART THREE

A SPIRITUAL LAUNCHING PAD

ten

Stomach Grumblings

I am a champion. A winner. The best of the best.

It started when I was in kindergarten and the time came for the end-of-year awards ceremony. I sat crisscross applesauce on the colored linoleum tiled floor, anxious to hear what certificate I would take home to hang proudly on the refrigerator. My teacher stood on the stage, announcing from the podium with great expression the character trait for which each student had been recognized. Pausing for effect, she waited just a moment before declaring the name of the privileged individual who possessed such talent and ability.

With each trait she announced, I held my breath and replayed the past year in my mind, hoping it was a quality that I had displayed.

"The Good Friend Award goes to . . ."

She named someone other than me. I had to support that decision when I remembered how I had pushed a girl down on the playground. Darn.

"The Best Handwriting Award goes to . . ."

Oh, how I wanted that one. My penmanship would make most mothers cry with pride. I was totally getting this one!

She named another child. I had to ratify that decision when I remembered all the assignments I had blitzed through in an attempt to be the first one finished in the classroom. Better luck next time.

Best Mathematician. Most Creative. Perfect Attendance. As each award went by my inner dialogue grew more and more frustrated. Did I have nothing to offer the world? Then came my moment.

"The Best Eater Award goes to . . . Erica Putzier!"

O. M. Gee. That's me! I won an award! I jumped to my feet and ran to the front of the room. Pride welled up in my little heart as I remembered finishing every meal I was ever served at school. No scraps here, no sir-ee. "Lick it clean" is my motto. *This is a major award.* I was being recognized for my appetite and I knew no one else could measure up. I felt like the father in *The Christmas Story.*

My mom stood at the back of the auditorium, shaking her head in disbelief, though she did well to hide it from me. With the level of determination I possessed even as a small girl, she knew this award spelled disaster. From then on, I would make it my goal to live up to my label. Would a champion eater leave the table after only one helping? Ha! Bring on the seconds! Bring thirds. Bring dessert. I was not afraid of a challenge. I vividly remember taco-eating competitions at Country Grandma's house in which I would eat as much as the grown men.

The next year brought the first-grade awards ceremony. I was ready. Best Handwriting? I scoffed at the mention of an award so puny. Anyone could perfectly craft letters. We were in first grade now. Hello? Were they handing out awards for breathing as well, because writing takes about the same amount of talent.

Eating, on the other hand, is a special endowment. Not everyone can become a master. I could not care less about other awards that year. Mine was already decided in my heart. When they called out my name this time, I knew what would follow.

"And for Erica Putzier, we have the award for . . . 'Best Eater!'" #nailedit

I can almost picture my mother's eyes burning a hole in the teacher as she spoke those words. Her daughter was already a healthy eater. Did they need to keep encouraging her to gorge herself? I was proud as I could be, displaying my certificate for all to see. I was a winner and no one could take that away. Well, nothing but a well-intended call to the school from my mother to request they let the champion retire that year by not awarding her title ever again. I was eating my family out of house and home.

A Fondness for Food

When I was a teenager no one believed I had a love affair with food because I am a tiny person. They questioned my allegiance to the mighty mealtime—until they saw me eat. I still get excited about the mere thought of food. I finish one meal and ask about our next meal. By now you, the reader, can testify to my obsession with food as evidenced by the number of parables about food found within these pages.

In my Christian walk, I never linked food with faith. They stood independent of each other, although they were not adversaries, just neighbors. Burgers had their own place and Jesus another. They did not mingle. Jesus did not ask to share my fries (He knows they are not made for sharing), and I did not offer. Stay in your lane, food.

When I met Joey, he offhandedly mentioned a particular friend who did not understand the purpose of fasting. I chuckled as if I knew all about fasting and was shocked his friend did not. What was his opinion on fasting? I was asking for a friend, of course. Joey told me about trading mealtime for God time. He would fast, skipping meals and using that empty space to intentionally spend time with God instead.

That's dumb, I thought. *I can be intentional with God any time, so why would I skip a meal to do it? Fasting doesn't make any sense.* I kept my thoughts from my new boyfriend and never brought it up again. Instead of digging more into what the Bible said about it, I pushed it out of my mind. I knew the Bible talked about fasting and I knew Jesus did it for forty days, but I failed to see how that should change my faith. Or my dinner.

I recognize the fact that God loves food. Food is not evil or bad. He made it for the main purpose of fueling our bodies. While animals are good pets and make our earth a happier place, one of their purposes is to feed us. God made animals and plants for us to eat: "Everything that lives and moves about will be food for you. Just as I gave you the green plants, I now give you everything" (Genesis 9:3).

The Bible is filled with stories of food and its connection to God. He uses manna to represent God's provision for His people. The body of Christ is represented by bread. Eating together is central to communion and community for believers. This is why churches have fellowship halls. I love this gift from our Creator, and I celebrate by eating medium rare steaks and baked potatoes loaded with butter and sour cream.

We can learn more about ourselves by studying our relationship with food: how we consume it, whether we love it or hate it, whether or not we have made it our god. We manipulate food to gain control when we are not in control. We indulge to celebrate or abstain to punish. The human connection with food runs deeper than we can imagine, and I would bet you feel its effects as strongly as I do. I have met very few people who are not invested in food, whether in a healthy or unhealthy way. I had been heavily invested in food for my whole life, but I was not sure if it was a good or bad thing.

I began to realize that God actually has an opinion about the food we put into our bodies, as well as when we do it.

I considered undertaking a fast—just entertaining the thought. *Surely it wouldn't be too difficult to try fasting for a bit and see what happens.* I scheduled a short one.

But the closer I got to the first day of the fast, the more anxious I became. What would I do about my morning coffee? Would it be weird if I had a lunch meeting and had to sit across the table from someone without a meal? What about cooking dinner for my family? How would I survive smelling it and not being able to partake? This fasting thing was turning out to be more than I had bargained for. Maybe food did have a hold on me that was stronger than was appropriate.

No one in my Christian circle talked about fasting, so I could not imagine that it did much good for anyone.

Then I started wondering, *Is there some secret society that I need to join that will teach me how to do it? What am I allowed to drink? How long do I abstain from food? One meal or the entire day? What about fasting one type of food, but not all food?*

Fasting Overview

"Fasting." It had to mean something to God or He would not have put it in the Bible as many times as He did. It must have

153

a purpose. I turned to the Good Book to see what it had to say about the subject.

A little research uncovered that fasting has different purposes for different situations. Fasting is about you, but it is also about God. Fasting is about groups of people, but also the individual. At the heart level, it represents surrender and trust. At the physical level, it embodies sacrifice and supply. At the heavenly level, it unleashes power and praise. Fasting is many things to many people, but you only need to concern yourself with what it means to you. Fasting is transformative. Your surrender, sacrifice and praise will never be sweeter nor your dependence on Him greater than when you choose to let go of what you love for His sake.

What are some of the purposes for fasting?

Fasting for Breakthrough

Then all the Israelites, the whole army, went up to Bethel, and there they sat weeping before the LORD. They fasted that day until evening and presented burnt offerings and fellowship offerings to the LORD.

Judges 20:26

God sent His people up against an army that they could not defeat; they lost every time. Before they went out for battle that next day, they fasted and worshiped God, praying He would move on their behalf. God gave them victory as a result.

Fasting for Direction

While they were worshiping the Lord and fasting, the Holy Spirit said, "Set apart for me Barnabas and Saul for the work to which I have called them." So after they had fasted and prayed, they placed their hands on them and sent them off.

Acts 13:2–3

The apostles heard what God had planned for Barnabas and Saul because they were fasting. Their ears were open to the plan God had for these men, and their obedience (sending them off) set into motion one of the greatest expansions of the Church in history.

Fasting as Worship

There was also a prophet, Anna, the daughter of Penuel, of the tribe of Asher. She was very old; she had lived with her husband seven years after her marriage, and then was a widow until she was eighty-four. She never left the temple but worshiped night and day, fasting and praying.

Luke 2:36–37

Fasting can be a part of our everyday worship. Continuously denying our needs reminds us God is our supplier. We can do nothing apart from Him, and that knowledge stimulates our worship.

Fasting for Answered Prayers

So we fasted and petitioned our God about this, and he answered our prayer.

Ezra 8:23

Want more powerful prayers? Try fasting. It is like a turbo-boost for your petitions. We can fast when we want God to move for someone and our words do not seem to be working.

Conversation with God, paired with fasting, works powerful supernatural changes.

Fasting to Mourn

They mourned and wept and fasted till evening for Saul and his son Jonathan, and for the army of the LORD and for the nation of Israel, because they had fallen by the sword.

2 Samuel 1:12

I have never yet used fasting to mourn, but I see it in God's Word more than once. I may try it someday when a sorrowful situation presents itself.

Fasting Corporately

Some people came and told Jehoshaphat, "A vast army is coming against you from Edom, from the other side of the Dead Sea. It is already in Hazezon Tamar" (that is, En Gedi). Alarmed, Jehoshaphat resolved to inquire of the LORD, and he proclaimed a fast for all Judah. The people of Judah came together to seek help from the LORD; indeed, they came from every town in Judah to seek him.

2 Chronicles 20:2–4

I am moved to tears by the concept of corporate fasts—when a church, city or people group commits to sacrifice together for the good of the whole. There is a powerful bond formed when people fast together, and it will not be easily broken.

Fasting for Repentance

"Even now," declares the LORD, "return to me with all your heart, with fasting and weeping and mourning."

Joel 2:12

Fasting can be part of your repentance before God, an earnest showing on your part of your broken heart for grieving God. The Holy Spirit reveals when your heart has wandered from God's will. Depending on how that wandering affected you, your repentance may result in a physical response, such as fasting.

A Shocking Revelation

As part of our church staff, I had regular conversations with women from our church about baptism. As a church, we reached out to those who were far from God, and we welcomed many people who had come to Christ for the first time. As a public profession of their faith, baptism was their next step after receiving salvation.

It was time for our staff to check in on those contemplating this important decision. How were they feeling? Did they have questions? Were they ready? I decided to fast for those who were searching their hearts and making such a life-changing decision.

My prayer to God sounded like this: *God, I am not sure what to expect from fasting. But I want to do what You ask us to do in the Bible, and I know fasting is an act of submission to You. I pray that You will show up big time for me and confirm that I am heading in the right direction in all of this. I'm asking You to prove the power of fasting by having someone step forward for baptism—someone I would never expect. Please show me that abstaining from food and humbling myself for you does something supernatural that I cannot explain.*

I had done my research. Learning how our fathers in the faith fasted regularly had been encouraging, but it was not enough to make me want to fast. This fast would be an act of simple obedience, a testing of the power of fasting. Would it measure up to what I had heard?

I had meetings lined up with women all week long, but I fasted Monday to jump-start God's work. From morning through evening, no food or drink except water. Any time my stomach grumbled, I prayed that prayer. I knew God was going to answer me, but I could not anticipate what it would look like. No one called me, frantically begging for baptism. My meetings the rest of the week were productive and a couple of women made decisions for Christ, but nothing happened that shocked me. Grateful for Jesus moving in their hearts, I rested in His sovereignty. Their decisions should be enough to satisfy my questions.

And then it happened.

My early morning prayer time was especially powerful. I was still pleading for God to move in a way I had not experienced. There had to be big reasons behind this call to fast or I would not have felt such hesitation, right? As I prayed, God asked a humbling question. He very clearly asked me, *How can you ask all these women you lead to do something you have never done?*

You see, I had accepted Jesus as a teen at summer camp. There was no baptism that followed since our family did not go to church. When we did begin attending church a year later, I never thought to ask for baptism from our pastor. I went from high school to college, leading ministries and worship. I knew baptism was not going to save my soul, so it never felt urgent. And besides, I "publicly professed" my faith each week as I served in leadership. The world knew about my faith, and baptism seemed to be an unnecessary step. Yet here I was, an employee of the church, teaching on the importance of a baptism I had never experienced.

Mine was the baptism no one expected.

Oh my. I certainly was not prepared for that one. I was anxious about going through with it. What would people think? Would every parent revolt, thinking that I had been ministering to their children without myself being a Christian? It would mean admitting to the entire church I had waited almost twenty years to get baptized. I worried that my boss and pastor would be concerned about others' opinions and would tell me to get baptized privately. I, too, wanted to do it privately. God said no. I wanted to have just my family in attendance. God said no. He told me not to be ashamed or embarrassed. I was to be obedient.

That Sunday I stood in front of the entire congregation and shared my story—the fasting, the challenge I laid out to God and how He answered my challenge with my own obedience. Then Joey baptized me. I emerged from the water to the sound of applause.

Fasting had moved mountains I had not known about. Fasting had opened my eyes to an area of my faith that I had not allowed to develop. It gave me the courage to follow through with what God revealed was my personal next step. It tuned my heart to hear from Him better than ever before.

How to Fast

Whether you fast from food or media, sugar or meat, God will welcome any sacrifice. I have found in my own journey that God will ask me to give up different things for different seasons. He wants me to fast faithfully in response to Him, not because of a rigid schedule.

When I first tried it, He asked me to fast once a week. On Sunday, I would pray that He would reveal which day I was to cut out all food and He would always answer. Sometimes it was on days when it would be easy to fast, other times not so much. But I did not choose—He did.

In other seasons, He has asked me to give up coffee for thirty days. I have gone for weeks without a prompt to fast at all. God does not want legalism in fasting. He wants a fresh response from a current word. Just because you have fasted every Monday for the past twenty years does not mean that is what He desires for your next twenty.

Fasting is personal and uniquely different for each of God's children. How you fast, when you fast and what you fast from are between you and God. Again, there is no rule book on the specifics, only examples of those who did it in the Bible. One thing we do know—

Do not be a whiny baby about it.

Put on a Happy Face

> When you fast, do not look somber as the hypocrites do, for they disfigure their faces to show others they are fasting. Truly I tell you, they have received their reward in full. But when you fast, put oil on your head and wash your face, so that it will not be obvious to others that you are fasting, but only to your Father, who is unseen; and your Father, who sees what is done in secret, will reward you.
>
> Matthew 6:16–18

We see from this passage of Scripture that Jesus *expected* His followers to fast. He says "when" you fast, not "if" you fast. Fasting was considered a common practice. We can also gather that some people put on one-man theatrical performances when they fasted, so everyone would appreciate their suffering. "O, woe is me, I am so holy." (*Gimme a break, Steve. I saw you sneak extra servings of Martha's cheesecake last night. I think you're gonna pull through.*)

I believe it is in a misinterpretation of this Scripture to say you are never to tell anyone about your fast, ever. Sometimes my friends whisper as if they are cussing when they share that they are fasting. Sure, you do not need to shout it out or brag about your endeavors, but if information needs to be shared for the sake of the group, there is no harm in that.

For example, Joey loves to surprise me with coffee and breakfast on mornings when I write. I find that if I do not tell him the night before that I plan to fast, he will make me breakfast—which I will have to give to the kids. (Believe me, no one wants a coffee-drinking five-year-old.) As I see it, telling him that I am fasting is a courtesy, not bragging.

Or how about a day when you are going to lunch with a friend and God springs on you that morning you will not be eating all day? I like to be considerate of my friend and offer to reschedule if she will feel weird about me staring at her while she eats. It does not bother some people, but it does others. Being a good friend, I ask.

The other times I share about fasting are when I feel prompted to do so by the Holy Spirit. I cannot help but think how much sooner I would have started fasting if someone had only opened a dialogue with me about it. We should not be so afraid of sinning by talking about our fasting. This fear may be one of the reasons it has become a taboo subject, even in church. I have found that my openness to share my struggles or victories in fasting can be a way to help others be willing to try it. It works both ways. Ask others what they do when they fast—how long, what they give up, how it has changed their life. Begin the dialogue and watch your own faith for fasting grow.

It's All about the Heart

Whatever timeline, whatever method, whatever sacrifice you bring before God, make sure your intentions are pure. "People look at the outward appearance, but the Lord looks at the heart" (1 Samuel 16:7). Fasting will open you to a new level of dependence on God for all your needs. In addition, He can rid you of your headaches from not drinking caffeine all day. He can supply you with energy to chase your toddler. He can even help you not get hangry.

The truth is that our God is all we will ever need, even when our grumbling stomach disagrees.

Check Your Pulse

1. What is your personal experience of fasting?

2. Jesus wants His followers to fast regularly. How can you begin to work fasting into your schedule? What scares you about going without food?

3. What kinds of conversations have you had about fasting? What kinds of conversations would you like to have? Ask God to arrange some interactions with others on this topic.

4. What is the one thing you hope to gain from your sacrifice? What new revelation or relationship are you hungry for in your walk with God?

5. Ask God right now when you should fast next and what He wants you to lay down. Then do it.

eleven

Who Untied My Bowtie?

As a high schooler I had heard talk of "speaking in tongues," but I did not know much about it. I was taught it was a gift that God gave the early Church to spread the Gospel to other nations. My church explained that on the day of Pentecost, as recounted in the second chapter of the book of Acts, the disciples had spoken in various languages because the Holy Spirit wanted them to speak God's message in the languages of the people in the crowd, even though they themselves could not understand what they were saying. I was told that this miraculous gift no longer existed and that, furthermore, someone speaking in tongues would never utter an unknown language that would sound like gibberish to hearers. Not only was it a dead gift, it was something that should be guarded against.

Okay. Got it.

I am good at following rules.

Remember that time God showed up in the prophetic word that a stranger spoke over me? As it turned out, that woman prayed in tongues. Often. This caused me great confusion. How could she do something so against God, yet hear Him clearly enough to share life-changing truths with me? It failed to line up. Not that I expected her to be perfect, but I knew her well enough to recognize that nothing in her personality would cause her to make up a "prayer language" for show. This made me stop and question the teaching from my teen years.

She was not the only one who caused me to pause. The more time I spent around women in leadership who were speaking so much truth to me, the more I realized how many of them had a prayer language. These were normal ladies: solid, intelligent, godly, gifted women. I had always thought of people who spoke in tongues more in terms of the cartoonish Cruella de Vil—out-of-control crazy, with a gag-worthy fashion sense. Was praying in tongues a real spiritual gift? I had some digging to do.

I was referred to a book called *The God I Never Knew*, by Robert Morris, a pastor I trusted. That book title summed up my whole life up to that time, which was in an I-never-knew condition. I was skeptical, but I was open to learning as well. I started poring over Bible verses, researching commentaries and sermons and googling anything related to "prayer languages" and "speaking in tongues."

I really could not understand how words could come out of my mouth that I did not first think in my own mind. How could this be? It seemed ridiculous to be able to speak a language I had never learned by somehow bypassing the language centers of my brain. Surely this was all pretend, some kind of a charismatic Christian freak show. God did not need people's help to look more spectacular. Why were they trying to embellish His power and beauty?

My heart grew heavy with unanswered questions, so I asked my trusted friend to share her journey of receiving her prayer language. I knew her well and her motives were always pure. She described her prayer language in a way that I had never heard. Turns out she did not enjoy speaking in her prayer language. In fact, she had been alarmed when God first asked her to speak out that way. Besides being held back by fear, she had no desire to be acknowledged for her "gift." Nevertheless in humility she had offered her voice for God to use whenever and however He deemed appropriate.

Wow. I had always assumed anyone speaking a prayer language (if it was even real) would delight in others' attention. "Pride!" scoffed the girl who might have admitted that she had a lot to learn, but who felt she knew it all about prayer. I had never imagined that this gift was about surrender and not control.

I tucked these things away and pondered them in my heart, like Mary, Jesus' mother.

Steer the Ship

I was deeply hungry for God. Searching, my heart began to crave more knowledge of God on an intimate level. More of His Spirit. More, more, more. I was no longer satisfied with the shallow end of spiritual experience. I had experienced a taste of the deep end and it had opened my eyes. I am nothing if not researched, so off I went to hunt for more.

I sought out the wisdom of a mentor of mine, someone I knew believed in a spiritual prayer language. I tried to explain my conundrum, bumbling and second-guessing myself. In response, she pointed me to James 3:2–4.

> We all stumble in many ways. Anyone who is never at fault in what they say is perfect, able to keep their whole body in check. When we put bits into the mouths of horses to make them obey us, we can turn the whole animal. Or take ships as an example.

Although they are so large and are driven by strong winds, they are steered by a very small rudder wherever the pilot wants to go.

So, who was my pilot?

I had given my whole life to Jesus, so why would I not give over complete control to the one steering the ship? I had prayed for God to guide my words for years, but mainly so that they would not be unwise or unkind. It never crossed my mind to ask God to take *actual* control of my tongue, rather than merely influencing it for the better. What if I allowed the Holy Spirit to speak a language through me that my mind could not comprehend or control?

James goes on to write: "Likewise, the tongue is a small part of the body, but it makes great boasts. Consider what a great forest is set on fire by a small spark" (verse 5). In a positive sense, what if one of my sparks would be surrendering what I thought prayer should look like? What would change if I became less concerned with the language and more concerned with the outpouring? This could be the very component that would set my faith on fire. Could the future of my faith depend upon one of the smallest members of my body? Had I wasted hours and months and years trying to control the very thing that should control me?

God would not call me to control my tongue and not give me a means to do so. He wanted to steer my ship. The words I say, the language I use, the evil that comes out of my mouth—all of it could be redeemed. My heart was made new when I accepted Christ. Why not now my tongue?

My many questions were beginning to resolve themselves. As it began to make more sense to me, I was getting less nervous about the concept of a prayer language. Logically, I was beginning to realize that it actually made more sense that God should control our tongue than not.

The Corinthians Argument

The biggest chunk of Scripture that describes speaking in tongues can be found in two chapters of the book of 1 Corinthians. Let's begin with chapter 12.

> Now to each one the manifestation of the Spirit is given for the common good. To one there is given through the Spirit a message of wisdom, to another a message of knowledge by means of the same Spirit, to another faith by the same Spirit, to another gifts of healing by that one Spirit, to another miraculous powers, to another prophecy, to another distinguishing between spirits, to another speaking in different kinds of tongues, and to still another the interpretation of tongues. All these are the work of one and the same Spirit, and he distributes them to each one, just as he determines.
>
> 1 Corinthians 12:7–11

> Now you are the body of Christ, and each of you is a part of it. And God has placed in the church first of all apostles, second prophets, third teachers, then miracles, then gifts of healing, of helping, of guidance, and of different kinds of tongues. Are all apostles? Are all prophets? Are all teachers? Do all work miracles? Do all have gifts of healing? Do all speak in tongues? Do all interpret?
>
> 1 Corinthians 12:27–30

Speaking in tongues as referred to in verse 7 is a gift given to the church body to serve the common good. These gifts are intended to be exercised in the church body as a means of building up believers. The first time the gift of tongues was used for the common good was on what is known as the "birthday of the Church" (see Acts 2) when the apostles received the Holy Spirit and began to speak in the many native tongues of those standing near them, though they did not know the languages themselves. It was a miracle of communication that no person could make happen, only God. Thousands came to believe in Christ that day, because of the power the gift displayed.

We do not know how the language translation happened, whether in the mouths that spoke out in the languages of those listening or in the ears of the hearers who may have interpreted the languages as their own. Either way, the message was received loud and clear.

Since that day, there have been many documented cases that are similar, for instance when missionaries are gifted to preach to a tribe or group of people whose language they do not speak. The people listening can hear and understand every word spoken.

The funny thing is, the focus of these verses in 1 Corinthians is not on validating the gifts. The purpose is to prove the unity of the Spirit in the Church, in which all parts of the body work together for the good of its people. The gift of tongues is referred to in the same list as teaching and helping, and no one argues about the value of those gifts. Why debate tongues so heavily?

Mostly because we do not like the unexplainable.

It gets even more unexplainable. What do we do with comments such as this one from the next chapter of the letter to the Corinthians? "If I speak in the tongues of men or of angels, but do not have love, I am only a resounding gong or a clanging cymbal" (1 Corinthians 13:1).

Two kinds of languages are implied: tongues of men and tongues of angels. Acts 2 describes tongues of men, because men were able to understand every word spoken. But what are tongues of angels? We read about angels speaking throughout both the Old Testament and the New, but the nature of their speech is not specified. Here special angelic language is implied; these heavenly beings speak a heavenly language, or languages. This verse declares that Christians can speak in either language.

But in actual fact, language is not the focus of these verses— love is. First Corinthians 13 is Paul's famed love chapter. He was not responding to a debate about the validity of the gift of tongues. Instead, he was leading a discussion of unity and love within the church, with particular emphasis on the appropriate motive behind the use of any of the spiritual gifts. Was the person speaking in the unknown language doing so in love? Or did it serve as a disruption?

Although the early Church was not debating the validity of this one little gift, we divide denominations because of it. I dare say the gift of tongues is one of the least of all God has to offer, yet we lose friendships over it. How can we begin to conduct civil discussions and stop labeling each other as ungodly?

It can be too hot to handle. No wonder I knew nothing about the gift of tongues; as I grew up in the church, no one had been brave enough to bring it up and have an open-minded conversation about it. Salvation does not depend upon the gift of tongues one way or the other, yet we get worked up about it. Maybe, just maybe, God is bigger than our textbook understanding of Him.

The Real Deal

One night, God would not let me sleep. I tossed and turned, tossed and turned, until He finally had my attention.

God, I'm pretty tired. I don't want to be a sleepy lunatic with my children tomorrow. Let's get on with it. What do you want from me?

Come pray, He said.

I complained under my breath (just a tiny bit) and dragged my feet into the living room. It was cozy and warm and comforting.

I knelt with my face on the carpet, a usual position for me when seeking God. I began by declaring His work in my life and thanking Him for His goodness. My prayers evolved into asking for insight and healing for friends, which resulted in crying out for more of Him. I no longer cared what it might look like; I wanted more. I wanted to go deeper. My life needed to be different. It needed fresh light and a refreshing that only He could give.

In my Spirit and in my heart, I said, *God, I don't know what this "prayer language" is all about. But everything in me is crying out for more. I don't have adequate words to express this emotion that is as deep as my marrow. If you want me to experience this gift, I receive it.*

I did not realize it at first, but my prayer had opened the door for Him to move. He did not kick the door in; I had to invite Him first.

Immediately, I heard a syllable in my head.

Fah.

What, God?

Fah.

I do not understand, God. What does that mean?

Just open your mouth and say it: "Fah."

Alone, in the silence of my living room, I sat up. I raised my eyes to heaven and I opened my mouth, shaping the sound, "fah." And the rest just poured out effortlessly. Words I had never heard before began cascading out of my mouth. For a few minutes my mouth and tongue were totally surrendered.

Then I stopped.

Wow. What just happened?

It started when I asked. It stopped when I stopped it. I did not know I could stop it.

I sat and prayed silently, in English, still wondering what exactly had taken place. As I prayed in my mind, I felt that spiritual prayer language rise up again in my spirit, this time stronger. I opened my mouth and it came again. I was not done. Unsure how to react, I thanked God for making it real for me. I thanked Him for being patient while I searched for answers to my questions. I was honored to receive the gift and I was going to use it.

I had crossed into the next level of my faith. Though I did not know what I believed about every theological detail of what had just happened, I felt girded up in my faith and strengthened. He had told me what to say and I had said it. He did the rest. No one was around to judge me. I had not done it to impress anybody. There was no one coaching me through it. It was just me and God having a conversation. He could not have picked a better setting for a skeptic like me to receive this gift.

Growing in the Gift

As with any gift God gives us, we must exercise it. The more we exercise it, the stronger it becomes.

I began to pray in the Spirit any time I was alone. My vocabulary of a few sounds and phrases turned into a fluent-sounding language. Just as a baby stumbles over words and syllables in the beginning, I felt my way through the way phrases formed in my mouth. It was different from my English language.

After the language developed more, inflections and volume came, just as in a normal language spoken fluently. Often my prayer language had a bold, stern sound. It could also be gentle and whisper-like. It was exciting to grow in this mysterious gift. I still did not understand it, but now I knew it was real. I did not know the words I was praying, nor did I understand what I was praying for. When I found these verses, I took them to heart:

Since you are eager for the gifts of the Spirit, try to excel in those that build up the church. For this reason, the one who speaks in a tongue should pray that they may interpret what they say. For if I pray in a tongue, my spirit prays, but my mind is unfruitful. So what shall I do? I will pray with my spirit, but I will also pray with my understanding; I will sing with my spirit, but I will also sing with my understanding.

1 Corinthians 14:12–15

Those verses described me; I was hungry for His gifts but I also wanted to know what I was praying. I prayed for God to give me an understanding of my words.

Your Sin Can Keep Away a Gift

Joey had longed to speak in tongues for years. He had grown up in a church that did not believe in the gift, but once he learned about it from a friend, he desired it. At every prayer conference, he went to the front in response to the invitation to receive the gift of tongues. He was told to move his mouth and make sounds until it came out.

Nothing.

Earlier, he and his friends used to make fun of people who spoke in tongues. The joke was that you could recite, "Who untied my bowtie?" quickly over and over and pretend it was tongues. As the boys joked and laughed, they failed to realize the damage they were doing to their ability to receive the gift.

As an adult, Joey reflected back on his history of wanting the gift but never getting it, making fun of it, then forgetting about it all together. He asked God, "Why don't I have a gift I have asked for so many times?"

God spoke to his heart: *I am not going to give you a gift you ridiculed. You need to repent.*

Repent he did. Later, as he prayed aloud for someone, he started to feel that he might choke on his words. Then he felt that he was going to cough, but instead of a cough, a new language came out. God had given him the gift once he confessed the sin that stood in the way.

Words and Visions and Feelings—Oh, My!

God began to answer my prayer for understanding about what I was saying in my prayer language.

For example, one day I was ministering to someone in prayer and I was praying in the Spirit. I started to hear words in my mind that were not the same as the words I was speaking. As I continued to pray, I would get more words. *Protect. Revive. Heal her pain.* It took me a minute to understand that God was giving me an understanding of what my spirit was praying in my prayer language. Awesome.

Then visions started to come, strongly. I saw huge angelic soldiers in the room, surrounding those of us who were praying. Another time, I saw a large golden fence that reached higher than I could see. One time I saw honey (a biblical symbol of blessing and delight) pouring down over my friend as she led worship. It sounds crazy, but I know it was not just my imagination. I believe the Holy Spirit was showing me the spiritual realm and what I was praying for.

Sometimes the revelation came by way of feelings—not light, easygoing emotions, but rather the whole gamut of deep passions. Sometimes profound sadness escaped my throat in sobs and wails. Other times I felt boundless joy that could not be contained, and I laughed harder than I had in a long time.

I am so glad I pursued God's gifts—and that He pursued me. Now I want everyone to know how beautiful and powerful praying in the Spirit can be. I find it breathtaking to see how God uses His gifts to grow His people. Throughout all of my searching, this one discovery has been the biggest catalyst for my bold faith.

Check Your Pulse

1. What do you think about the Scripture verses presented in this chapter? To be objective, you may need to identify and perhaps lay down your preconceived notions and what you have been taught in the past about speaking in tongues.

2. How do you allow God to direct the words you speak? How do you let Him steer the ship?

3. How has your skepticism or lack of reverence held you back from receiving more from God?

4. If you have a prayer language, describe your experience receiving it for the first time. If you have not received this gift, have you asked for it? Why or why not?

5. Does something stand in the way of freedom in your own prayer language? Doubt? Fear? Timidity? Confess it before God and pray for a fresh filling of His Spirit.

twelve

Healing

We had come to Colorado for a short vacation. Nestled deep in the small valley of Lake City, surrounded by the mountains, I was finding my soul's song in the cool breeze and the soft falling rain. This was heaven. A river wound through tall pine trees nearby. From our windows we could hear it rushing over rocks. As I settled in at my friend's cozy guest apartment, I was hit with a vision of oil pouring over my hands as I prayed over a home. It was just a quick image, but significant enough to get my attention.

At this point in my life, these images were not uncommon. I asked God to reveal what it meant and then moved on through my day. The same image came back a few times, but with no explanation. I knew He would get my attention when the time was right and that He would show me what to do. (He and I were tight like that. #bffs)

The next day I spent hours chatting with my hostess on her front porch while our kids played together. Playdates save vacations. We were soaking up our whine-free time, sharing stories of how God had been moving in each of our lives. Such an encouraging friendship is a beautiful gift, not easy to find. As she began another story of how God was moving in her mountain village, she stopped mid-sentence and declared, "You need to pray over my friend's home. Her little boy needs healing desperately."

Cue oil vision.

I love it when God gives me a heads-up about something that He has planned.

I confirmed for her that yes, I was going to pray over this home and the boy, and that God had already shown me it would happen. God had just used the buddy system—I got the vision and she got the words. The kingdom of God is all about playing our part, and she and I had woven effortlessly together in ours.

She shared this little boy's story with me. Her friend Katie was desperate for answers for her five-year-old son, Dax. He had been born with complications and they were warned he could have problems as he grew. After facing various other obstacles, he began to have pain in his knees. It was serious pain, pain that caused him to scream out and cry. Yet no one could figure it out or ease it. It was torture for Katie to sit by and watch this. Fear crept into her heart as she worried about the "complications later in life" that the doctors had warned her about.

The frequency increased. What used to happen about once a month for a short period of time was now occurring three times a week for hours at a stretch. Little Dax would cry and hold his knees, begging for it to stop. In desperation about his worsening condition, his mother scheduled an appointment with a specialist. She knew God could heal him but she found it hard to see how.

To document the extent of his pain, she made a video on her phone of him in the midst of an episode. When I saw the video of Dax crying, I knew this was no joke. He was very much in real pain. We knew what God had asked us to do: pray.

Watching God Work

Katie's family lived above the small restaurant they owned in town. It was like a small slice of Texas in the state of Colorado. They served up home cookin' and deep-fried everything. They had purchased the building and had been remodeling it, board by board.

Five of us—Joey and I, our hostess Jess, and a friend named Billy and his brother—all climbed the steep outdoor steps alongside the restaurant. Our meeting with the family was very ordinary. Little Dax stood in the living room, sweet as could be. Katie sat on the floor and had Dax sit in her lap. We all laid hands on them. Joey and Billy laid their hands on Dax's knees, I had my hands on Katie's back and the others sat nearby.

As Joey began to pray out loud for healing, I immediately felt my prayer language rising up in my chest, so I quietly began to pray in whispers, doing battle in my spirit. Dax sat completely still, not moving a muscle. His mom sat praying silently, tears streaming down her cheeks. Joey felt led to ask Jess to pray over her friend. She laid hands on Dax and prayed brokenly amid sobs, pleading for complete healing.

We finished by praying over the entire house and quietly departed. It was then we heard what had happened as Joey prayed.

"Did you feel that?" Billy asked Joey. "His knees. Did you feel all the popping and shifting? Dax was not moving a muscle, but his knees were snapping under my hands!" Joey confirmed he had felt it and that Dax had not moved but the tendons and muscles in his knees had. In that moment of awe, we wondered if God had been healing Dax in the very moment our prayers

177

were being spoken. No matter what came next, we knew God had moved.

A month later Dax underwent testing to see if his condition had indeed caused the pain in his knees (the pain that he was no longer experiencing). The test results were negative. Nothing was wrong. Dax had been healed, and he has not had one day of pain in his knees since then.

Katie shared with me later what God had done in her home:

> I wanted to thank y'all for coming to pray over our house and my son! I know God sent y'all here to battle for us. God knew I needed warriors to stand with me. Since y'all left, my house is peaceful. My house is full of joy. My kids aren't fighting like they were. There are no more bad dreams and we are all sleeping so well. My husband and I are drawing closer and seeking Him together! The discontent is gone. I truly believe my son is healed. Praise God!

Laying On of Hands

> Is anyone among you sick? Let them call the elders of the church to pray over them and anoint them with oil in the name of the Lord. And the prayer offered in faith will make the sick person well; the Lord will raise them up. If they have sinned, they will be forgiven. Therefore confess your sins to each other and pray for each other so that you may be healed. The prayer of a righteous person is powerful and effective.
>
> James 5:14–16

God tells us to pray for healing by laying our hands on each other. Each individual needs to learn how God is calling him or her to play a part.

In my case, God shows me the people He wants me to lay hands on for healing. I do not pick and choose; He highlights them. He gives me a vision or a physical reaction when I see or hear that person. He shows me in my mind where my hands should touch, or He tells me in words. Often my body gets super-hot. My hands sometimes shake. My prayer language rises up—or I cannot speak at all. (This is how it happens for me personally, not how it works for everyone.)

My prayers for healing are not effective every time. I cannot make faith rise up in the person needing healing, just as they cannot make God heal them. We are at the mercy of God's timing and purpose. But we can pray with boldness any time we approach His throne.

My friend Patricia mentioned one day that her back was hurting. As soon as she said that, I got a tickle up the back of my neck and my heart started beating uncontrollably. This was how I knew the Holy Spirit wanted me to lay hands on her. (Other people had shared prayer requests that day, but hers was the only one like that.) I closed my eyes and prayed over her, moving my hands to any part of her back and neck God showed me in my mind. She texted me the next day to tell me she had been healed from her pain. Also that I had touched areas of her back that had been painful for years but that no one knew about. Every bit of pain was gone.

My friend Dori attended my retreat and received prayer to heal her infertility. Sixteen months later, she gave birth to a healthy new baby. At that same retreat, my friend Sarah asked for healing of her knee. After prayer, she was immediately healed and was able to kneel on the concrete minutes later without a hint of pain.

My good friend Danielle suffered from intense arthritis. I prayed over her and the pain was almost completely gone over the next few weeks, but it came back. She went to see more specialists. She prayed more prayers. She changed her diet. God revealed unconfessed sin in her heart. Slowly but surely, she has received the healing she prayed for.

Pick and Choose

Healing comes in a variety of ways. Whether it happens instantly or by means of a slow process, it is always wonderful and valuable.

Why does God heal some people and not others? I do not know. He picks and chooses, and we may only understand His reasons when we see Him face-to-face. One healing happens immediately, while others take time. Yet another person is never healed. I prayed my most earnest prayers for my mom to be healed from lung cancer, yet she passed away six months after her diagnosis. I have prayed for complete strangers who walked away healed.

Where is the justice? Do God's people get to win? Good, holy, amazing people pass away every day in the midst of horrific circumstances, yet others who are dishonest or even murderers receive healing and protection. It does not compute in our earthly minds.

Unpredictable and confusing as it is, we are called to use the gift of healing if we have it. Ultimately, we must trust in God's sovereignty and goodness, no matter the outcome.

In the Bible accounts, we see Jesus walk past many sick people to choose one specific person to heal. How could He narrow it down to a single person like that? How was it part of God's sovereign plan? Did it depend on the faith of the person who needed healing? Did God's timing ultimately determine why they were healed at that moment and not days, months, or years earlier?

It is easy to get caught up in the what-ifs and whys of healing. Should I even bother to ask if this is not God's perfect time? What if it is His will for this person to be healed in another way? Do I even have the gift of healing? Can I be effective without it? So many questions.

For my part, I would rather storm the gates of sickness than sit in my questions. Desperation for healing must supersede the hesitation that my questions produce. I throw off anything that hinders me and fully trust that God is working all things for the good of His people. I rest in God's sovereignty while I pray with unshakable faith that He is for us and not against us.

Absolute Faith

When praying for healing, you must believe and not doubt. Doubt can cripple the mighty works that God wants to do.

> Truly I tell you, if anyone says to this mountain, "Go, throw yourself into the sea," and does not doubt in their heart but believes that what they say will happen, it will be done for them.
>
> Mark 11:23

Do not doubt. Believe what you read in God's Word. Healing happens! Jesus healed people:

> Jesus went throughout Galilee, teaching in their synagogues, proclaiming the good news of the kingdom, and healing every disease and sickness among the people.
>
> Matthew 4:23

His disciples healed people:

> So they set out and went from village to village, proclaiming the good news and healing people everywhere.
>
> Luke 9:6

All of us find ourselves wondering at times if we truly believe in the healing power of God. Do we think God can heal through our hands, or is it reserved for the Supers? I believe the Bible is very clear that God gifts His children in many ways, and healing is one of them. The catch? You must believe in the gift to receive it. God will not force you to heal others. You must desire the gift. How can you heal someone without believing it can happen?

I know we already talked about the book of Corinthians in chapter 11, but I cannot address healing without reviewing those verses:

> Now to each one the manifestation of the Spirit is given for the common good. To one there is given through the Spirit a message of wisdom, to another a message of knowledge by means of the same Spirit, to another faith by the same Spirit, to another gifts of healing by that one Spirit, to another miraculous powers, to another prophecy, to another distinguishing between spirits, to another speaking in different kinds of tongues, and to still another the interpretation of tongues. All these are the work of one and the same Spirit, and he distributes them to each one, just as he determines.
>
> 1 Corinthians 12:7–11

The people of the church at Corinth had never seen the average Joe do the work that God had empowered the disciples to do. Paul was helping them to understand that God wanted to use everyone, and that His Spirit would give them gifts so that they could participate in His work.

> Now about the gifts of the Spirit, brothers and sisters, I do not want you to be uninformed. You know that when you were pagans, somehow or other you were influenced and led astray

to mute idols. Therefore I want you to know that no one who is speaking by the Spirit of God says, "Jesus be cursed," and no one can say, "Jesus is Lord," except by the Holy Spirit. There are different kinds of gifts, but the same Spirit distributes them. There are different kinds of service, but the same Lord. There are different kinds of working, but in all of them and in everyone it is the same God at work.

1 Corinthians 12:1–6

The Holy Spirit is God, part of the Trinity. We have access to Him whenever we need Him. He gives us the spiritual gifts we need to function in the body of Christ. Different gifts, one Spirit. It is not just the normal-seeming stuff that is "of God" while the weirder stuff is "of the devil." The Holy Spirit gives all the gifts. The gifts are meant for everybody, not just certain extra-spiritual people.

I have seen with my own eyes—even by my own hands—the healing described by the Bible. I no longer doubt the gift of healing nor the purpose of God in healing His people. I embrace it wholeheartedly.

Spiritual Healing vs. Physical Healing

My sweet friend Courtney was infertile. Specialists could not pinpoint why she could not get pregnant after three and a half years of trying. Nothing worked: test after test, treatment after treatment. It made no sense. She and her husband, Christopher, were deemed perfectly healthy. There was no reason she should not be pregnant by now.

They had gone through tremendous changes that year. Chris had accepted Christ and had been transformed by his newfound faith. They were now making deliberate choices to follow God in every decision they made as a couple. When trying to conceive naturally did not work, they began to consider their options: in vitro fertilization? Adoption? Neither option felt right to them, so they did the only thing they could do: wait.

I was scheduled to speak at a local Moms of Preschoolers group and I was praying about whom I should bring with me as a support and prayer buddy. I heard Courtney's name in my spirit.

No, God. I am not bringing my barren friend to a room full of pregnant and very fertile women. It would make me the worst friend in the world! Can you imagine? "Thanks for joining me, Courtney. Enjoy the next two hours staring into the face of a dream you can't achieve. You're the best!" I can't do that.

God calmly replied, *She's the one to bring.*

So I invited her, kicking myself the whole time. Worst friend ever. How could I do this to someone I care about? She accepted because she is sweet and supportive, which made me feel worse. Then God told me the next detail.

You are going to share Courtney's story.

I was shocked. *Seriously? I don't have permission for that. I feel like I will be airing her dirty laundry in front of everyone. I have no right.*

Just ask permission.

During the entire car ride to the event I prayed for God to tell me if I should indeed share her story. The answer was clearly yes. Then He added this small, insignificant, no-big-deal detail:

Have the room of women pray for her womb to be healed.

I could not stop sweating or shaking. God was going to heal Courtney through the hands of women He has gifted with fertility? It would be a sign of His power to me, to Courtney and to a room full of women ripe with baby bellies. It all made sense now—why I should ask her to come, why I should share her story, why we should pray over her.

Still, it felt like a risk. God did not say He would heal her. He just said to pray. What would happen to Courtney's faith if nothing happened? What would those women believe about the power of God if we asked but failed to receive? How would I respond the next time God prompted me to pray for healing? I finally got brave enough to ask Courtney if I could share her story, and possibly pray over her if God led me to do so.

"Of course." As I mentioned, she is fantastically sweet.

I was tuned in to the Spirit more than ever that morning. I was not going to pray over Courtney unless He confirmed it for me. I shared with the women more in depth about God and His character than I had planned. This easygoing mom's group got a major dissertation on how faith works and how the power of God gets released by our bold prayers. I was passionate. Some women stared as if I had lost my mind, but I did not care. Truth is truth, and they needed to know that God does incredible work through our bold faith.

As I wrapped up the teaching, I paused and glanced toward Courtney sitting at a nearby table. *Is it yes or no, God?* I asked in my heart.

Yes.

I inhaled slowly and invited my friend to join me at the front. I began to tell everyone about her inability to conceive the baby she so desperately desired. I shared about her heartbreak and her disappointments. I shared about a God who cares for each of us and wants us to live in victory, not just in heaven, but here and now. How when we pray with bold faith, God will move in ways we cannot explain. I asked every woman in that room to lay hands on Courtney and pray in faith that God would heal her completely. There were so many of them that some had to lay hands on others who were touching Courtney.

I prayed aloud and then declared to the women in the room, "You will know that God is able to do all things when I call you to share that she is pregnant. Just wait and see. He is faithful."

Two months later, Courtney was pregnant.

Why had my friend not been healed the first time I prayed over her earlier that year? Why did God wait until that day in a room full of moms? Did her faith need to grow? Was He building the faith of a much bigger body of believers? We may never know.

Are You a Healer?

There is more than one way to receive God's gifts. For one, we can receive them through the hands of other believers who possess a particular gift already. God uses touch to transfer power and anointing. This is a deeply personal way for the people of the church to connect and grow together. Paul reminded Timothy of this truth: "For this reason I remind you to fan into flame the gift of God, which is in you through the laying on of my hands" (2 Timothy 1:6).

Or you can simply ask for the gift of healing. God can give you the ability to heal the sick when you ask in faith for more of His power in your life: "Therefore I tell you, whatever you ask for in prayer, believe that you have received it, and it will be yours" (Mark 11:24).

One thing is for sure: You will never know if God has gifted you with healing if you never think about it. You will never receive a gift unless you reach out in faith to receive it. And you will never grow in your exercise of any spiritual gift—especially a gift such as the gift of healing—unless you practice using it regularly.

Step out boldly and see what God will do.

186

Check Your Pulse

1. Look up the word *healing* in a concordance. Find all the instances in which God used His people to heal.

2. Many of the people of the world around us believe that healing through prayer is fake. What do you believe, and why?

3. The enemy plants doubts in your mind to keep you from being healed or from praying for someone else's healing. You can do something about that: Confess any doubts and ask for God to fill you with faith for His miracles.

4. Do you want the gift of healing? Have you asked for it? Why not ask now?

5. Many of us have experienced losing a loved one to sickness or have endured a physical impairment ourselves, which can cause hurt or anger toward God. Ask God to reveal any emotional healing you may need and receive His love.

thirteen

Dream a Little Dream

My husband sat up in bed one afternoon, jarred awake from his Sunday nap.

"I just had a dream that Josh and Sara were married."

He was talking about Josh, the current youth pastor at our church in Kansas City, and Sara, a girl who had been in our youth group in Florida years earlier. Sara was in college, studying to become a family counselor. We had stayed connected with her after we moved back to Missouri. I froze as Joey spoke those words. The two of them together? It was perfect!

"Joey, that is *genius*! How have we never thought to introduce them?"

Months later, Josh and Sara were dating. She moved to Kansas City to complete her degree. He asked her to marry him and she said yes. They now have a little boy and are doing ministry in Chicago.

All because of a dream on a lazy Sunday afternoon.

God, the Dream Weaver

Dreams are one of the unique and unusual methods that God uses to communicate with His people. Skeptics can easily shrug off spiritual dreams as the result of a late-night pizza binge or a walk down memory lane on Facebook, but not me. This was not the first prophetic dream my husband had experienced, nor was it the last.

Did his dream predict the future, or did the future come about because of the dream? I do not know, but I know God had His hand in it.

Some people are wary of dreams, thinking of them as spooky hocus-pocus or hoodoo-voodoo, best left to the spiritualists and psychics, but I believe that God desires to reclaim dreams as a gift for His people. However, we must be open to hear what He is trying to say through them. We must rekindle our curiosity to uncover the mysteries of Christ that can be found in the unexplainable world of dreams.

Indisputably God uses dreams and visions to communicate to His people; we see dreams all throughout the Old and New Testaments. How was the baby Jesus saved from the genocidal intent of King Herod? By a dream given to his father, Joseph. What was the cry of Pontius Pilate's wife as Jesus was presented for crucifixion? "Don't have anything to do with that innocent man, for I have suffered a great deal today in a dream because of him" (Matthew 27:19).

Over and over we see spiritual dreams in Scripture:

> "We both had dreams," they answered, "but there is no one to interpret them." Then Joseph said to them, "Do not interpretations belong to God? Tell me your dreams."
>
> Genesis 40:8

Now a young Hebrew was there with us, a servant of the captain of the guard. We told him our dreams, and he interpreted them for us, giving each man the interpretation of his dream.

Genesis 41:12

When there is a prophet among you, I, the LORD, reveal myself to them in visions, I speak to them in dreams.

Numbers 12:5–7

In the book of Acts we read what Peter said to the crowd after the disciples received the Holy Spirit:

Then Peter stood up with the Eleven, raised his voice and addressed the crowd: "Fellow Jews and all of you who live in Jerusalem, let me explain this to you; listen carefully to what I say. These men are not drunk as you suppose. It's only nine in the morning! No, this is what was spoken by the prophet Joel: 'In the last days, God says, I will pour out my Spirit on all people. Your sons and daughters will prophesy, your young men will see visions, your old men will dream dreams.'"

Acts 2:14–17

Peter was pointing out that God was unleashing His power on a new generation that would tell the story of His love and redemption in supernatural ways. It may seem a little crazy, but not to worry. He broke it down for them: "Guys. Don't freak out! God said weird stuff was gonna happen after He gave us His Spirit. Chill and take a deep breath, because strange languages, visions and dreams are all from God and a sign of His coming again someday. I'm not the first one to say this—my man Joel already told us this would happen. Welcome to the future."

I have always wondered why God chooses to speak to His people through dreams, which seem like such an unreliable source. Why can He not just tell us when we are awake? Why does the God of the universe choose to control our imaginations and allow us to experience Him on this level? I never believed dreams had significance—at least not *my* dreams. I could barely remember my dreams to begin with, let alone receive something revolutionary when I closed my eyelids.

Until one day, I did.

As I fell asleep one night, contemplating the gifts the Holy Spirit gives and the miraculous things I had witnessed recently, God reminded me of my dreamless state. Why had I never asked for spiritual dreams? I foolishly believed dreams were "Joey's thing" and that God had gifted me in different ways. I was okay with that.

Why not ask for one? God prompted my heart. What a fabulous idea. Why had I not asked for knowledge through whatever means He deemed appropriate, including dreams? Had I forgotten He is a good Father who gives good gifts? I accepted His invitation and prayed for a dream:

God, I know You give us good gifts. I want to surrender everything to You, even my mind, as I sleep. I am willing to be obedient if You want to give me a spiritual dream tonight. Help me remember it and make sure I understand that it is important. I will record it and share it as You show me. Amen.

Nothing fancy. I simply asked.

That night I had my first prophetic dream. I woke up early and God immediately said, *That was important.* I sat up and wrote down every detail I could remember, including the tiniest details, even the color of the walls and the emotions of people in the room.

Months later I was having dinner with a friend. As she shared about current events happening at our church, the Holy Spirit prompted me to share that dream. As I shared, my friend froze. She sternly told me to share my dream with our pastor. The dream that God had given me months prior became the confirmation for some major steps that were about to be taken in our church. I watched as details of my dream played out in real life.

God, who rules over the day and night, interrupts our earthly timeline to show us things to come. One of the ways the Holy Spirit tells us the future happens to be through dreams; we see it throughout the Bible. It is not "chance" or "coincidence" when dreams come to fruition, because it is one of God's supernatural ways of dispensing knowledge. We certainly cannot fake true prophetic dreams. We simply receive whatever He gives, however He gives it. What we do with these dreams matters.

Daniel the Dreamer

Daniel is one of my favorite dreamers in the Bible. His journey into prophetic dreams was much like mine and began with a simple ask. The Babylonian king, Nebuchadnezzar, had conquered Judah and taken its people captive. From among the captives, he chose the best of the best to train for service in his royal palace (like the *Top Gun* of the day, shirtless volleyball scene excluded). Among those chosen was the ruddy and handsome Daniel. This guy was the cat's meow, the cream of the crop. His buddies, whom we would later meet as Shadrach, Meshach and Abednego, were all handpicked by the king to continue in his service after their training was complete.

Poor King Nebuchadnezzar had a habit of not sleeping well. One night he had a dream that disturbed him but he could not remember the details. He summoned all the magicians, sorcerers, enchanters and astrologers in the kingdom to explain his dream. (I will refer to these men as the king's personal Magic Club from here on out, because #humor.)

If they failed to explain the dream, they would be chopped up into tiny pieces.

Geez, really? Apparently, Mr. King was Mr. Cranky Pants without his good night's sleep. The Magic Club was at a loss, but they were not going down without a fight. These magicians did what anyone facing a maniacal king would do: They stalled for time. They tried to convince the king that he was crazy to make that sort of request. No one in their right mind (cough, cough) would suggest that, right?

The king may have been cranky but he was not stupid, and he called them on their stalling tactics: "I am certain that you are trying to gain time, because you realize this is what I have firmly decided" (Daniel 2:8). Oops. Things are not looking good for our Magic Club as the king orders every one of them to be put to death.

Remember who had joined the ranks of the king's wise men? Our good buddy, Daniel. He had not been present when the others were summoned, but now the king's henchmen went looking for him. As they began to gather all the men who were to be executed by order of the king, Daniel negotiated with them to get face time with the king, and it worked.

He asked the king for one more day to receive revelation about the dream and it was granted. Dismissed by the king, Daniel ran home to the three amigos, Shadrach, Meshach and Abednego. The four men got on their knees before God and pleaded for His help. They needed vision, and they needed it fast.

God answered their prayers: "During the night the mystery was revealed to Daniel in a vision. Then Daniel praised the God of heaven" (Daniel 2:19). He makes it look so easy. Nicely done, Daniel—almost like a how-to example for hearing from God.

Since it was the middle of the night when he received the vision, we can pretty much assume that this is talking about a dream. In other words, in response to his request, God gave Daniel a dream so that he could interpret the king's dream.

The king asked Daniel,

"Are you able to tell me what I saw in my dream and interpret it?" Daniel replied, "No wise man, enchanter, magician or diviner can explain to the king the mystery he has asked about, but there is a God in heaven who reveals mysteries. He has shown King Nebuchadnezzar what will happen in days to come. Your dream and the visions that passed through your mind as you were lying in your bed are these:

"As Your Majesty was lying there, your mind turned to things to come, and the revealer of mysteries showed you what is going to happen. As for me, this mystery has been revealed to me, not because I have greater wisdom than anyone else alive, but so that Your Majesty may know the interpretation and that you may understand what went through your mind."

Daniel 2:26–30

Daniel presented the king with the only thing that could save his life: the one true God, the one who reveals mysteries. Daniel understood the opportunity he had to share his faith with the king and he did not shy away from it. He told the king everything that had been in the dream and interpreted each detail. No man could do this; the revelation came straight from God. This must truly be the real God, and now even the king knew it. His response was priceless.

Then King Nebuchadnezzar fell prostrate before Daniel and paid him honor and ordered that an offering and incense be presented to him. The king said to Daniel, "Surely your God is the God of gods and the Lord of kings and a revealer of mysteries, for you were able to reveal this mystery."

Daniel 2:46–47

Stewarding the Gift

We should never chase the gift of dreams so we can impress a king, our pastor or our friends. Once you have had a significant spiritual dream, you do not wave a flag over your home and proclaim what a great prophet you are or how wise your counsel is. Nothing about the gift is meant to bring glory to your own name; it is for the glory of a worthy God. The gift of dreams may feel fancy and special, but it is nothing without the Father's hand.

As we seek God first and the gift of love above all else, out of that love will arise a need for supernatural revelation. Sometimes God will send us that revelation in the form of a hard-to-understand dream. Who are we to turn our backs on what God offers if it happens to come in an unusual format?

We should never try to manipulate or manage prophetic dreams. Our part is to record the information the dreams reveal and to steward it. If you are new on this journey, here are some important points to remember:

Ask.

Have you ever asked for a dream from God? I had never done that. I think God was waiting for me to be intentional in seeking Him about my dreams before He gave them more significance. Until my heart was positioned to hear from Him while I slept, I would continue to miss out on what He had to offer.

Be humble.

Never clamor after a gift because it will make you look more holy. Instead, approach God in all humility, with the intention that whatever you receive will be used to make His name famous.

Also, never kick down doors or bust your way through to the front of the room to declare your revelation. Instead, seek His timing and His method of delivery in complete submission to Him.

Write it down.

The details of the dream matter. The emotions of the people in the dream, as well as your own while dreaming or when you awake, also matter. Even when you cannot describe the dream perfectly, write down the vibe or the general feeling. It is easy to forget a dream even just a few hours removed from it. Take time to write down every detail as soon as possible. It may seem overwhelming to get it all recorded, but it is worth it. Get as creative as necessary: Sketch pictures, make an audio recording, or write down the story line.

Ask for help.

Not remembering parts of your dream does not disqualify it from being used to bring revelation when needed.

The Bible tells us that the Holy Spirit helps us recall information (see John 14:26). Occasionally I cannot remember every detail of a dream. Did you know you can pray that God will bring it back to your memory? Then when you walk through a dream again, you can ask the Holy Spirit to highlight what matters. God will show you all you need to know.

Pray for an interpretation.

Your dreams may not make any sense to you. Whenever they seem unclear, always pray for clarity. God may or may not give it to you directly every time. He may send a trusted friend or mentor to interpret it. While the dream might not mean anything at the moment, it may after time and reflection. Either way, He will eventually help you interpret it; just ask Him.

Share or not to share?

Some dreams are for personal revelation only. Others are meant specifically for sharing. God will show you what to do with each significant dream. Pray for timing, delivery and specifics about whom it should be shared with.

Give credit where credit is due.

Just as Daniel received the dream and immediately praised God, so should we. Through dreams, God is talking to us in yet another way, and that should remind us not only of His glory and power but of His care for each of us individually. He uses dreams to bring us words of encouragement, correction and direction. What an undeserved honor, to be so well-loved by God Himself.

Come as Little Children

"Mom, I want to be bath-tized."

After watching many baptisms, Tristan was hopping at the chance to get dunked himself. Because we were a "church plant," we did not have traditional church fixtures—pews, air conditioning in the summer, or an official baptismal pool. When it came time to water-baptize our people, out came the colorful inflatable pool meant for kids. Grown adults had to kneel in order to get wet. But it was always exhilarating to see friends and family members enter into new life in Christ.

My heart holds warm memories of these moments in ministry. I remember the water dripping down their faces as new believers professed to everyone watching, "I believe in Jesus and He has changed me." It always took my breath away.

New life was not the only perk to baptism. I mentioned the fact that we had no air conditioning. Sweating after sitting indoors through a church service, we *all* wanted to get bath-tized. Kids, especially, because they could see it was just a little kiddie pool.

Tristan had asked before. Each time we had baptisms, my son would ask that same question: "Can I get bath-tized?" I always said no, knowing that he had not yet received Jesus as Lord. I would ask him,

"Are you a Christian, Tristan?"

"No."

"Then we will wait until you are. Until then, you can just go swimming in the pool after everyone leaves church today." And that became our routine on baptism days. He and his friends would take turns bath-tizing each other in the cold water after everyone else left. What better imaginary play could they choose? It got two thumbs up from this mama.

Fast-forward to two years later, after our move, in a new church.

Our children's pastor told us that our son had expressed interest in receiving Christ. I half-chuckled. Did they happen to have had a baby pool on stage when he said so? He was only seven years old. Did he truly grasp what salvation meant? How could his sweet baby heart understand justification, sanctification and atonement sacrifice? (When your parents attended Bible college, nothing about church comes easy, poor guy.)

We agreed to meet with our children's pastor. She walked Tristan through a list of questions to see if he understood what salvation entailed. It was amazing to watch him answer all the questions without hesitation. But reciting all the correct answers did not prove a heart change; head knowledge is not the same as heart knowledge. Can a seven-year-old even begin to comprehend something as deep as the cross?

By the end of our meeting, the children's pastor felt that Tristan was ready to take this next step. We were instructed to decide later that night if we felt he was ready. If so, we could lead him through the salvation prayer. This was encouraging, but I still felt a sense of reserve in my spirit. That evening, we decided to walk him through the prayer, coaching our son to learn what a prompt from the Holy Spirit felt like and reminding him that the prompt toward salvation was the most important one he would ever receive.

We gathered on his bed and began to ask questions. Why do you want to become a Christian? What do you think it means to go to heaven? What do you think about Jesus?

Tristan made it clear this was something he sincerely wanted to do. We held hands. His father led him through accepting Christ. The minute we opened our eyes, he smiled and said, "Now I get to go on the stage and sit in that tub. I bet it feels like a hot tub."

Sheez. Here we go again with the pool talk. I immediately regretted our decision. It was obvious that we had jumped the gun. It was just like that baby pool. I should have known better. I went to bed that night worried we had made a huge mistake. He was obviously too young. I worried he would be another church statistic. How many times in my years of ministry had I heard, "I accepted Christ as a young child but I don't remember it / it didn't mean anything / I was never really saved." I prayed intensely before I fell asleep that God would correct our mistakes.

I woke up early the next morning still heavy with worry. When my son woke up for school, he came running to me. "Mom. I had a really weird dream last night."

My ears perked right up. I knew this could be significant. Tristan never told me about his dreams, ever.

"I had a really scary dream. You, me and Dad were all there. I couldn't see very good—everything was really blurry. I kept rubbing my eyes, but it wouldn't get better. We were trying to climb a mountain together but we couldn't because there was a snake that was chasing us. It kept chasing us and chasing us and wouldn't stop. We would find a place to hide and he would find us every time. I was really scared! Then Dad stomped on the snake's head and killed it. Once he did that, I wasn't scared anymore and my eyes weren't blurry anymore. I could see everything. Then we all held hands and walked up the mountain together."

I sat completely still, in shock.

If this had happened six months earlier, I would have dismissed this dream as just another nightmare. But after all I had been experiencing with dreams personally, my spirit was ready to see the message God had for our family. Our prayer with Tristan for salvation was the right choice. He was truly a new creation in Christ!

In case you are feeling a little confused, here is a rundown of the dream:

- His vision is blurry because he had not yet accepted Christ.

  The god of this age has *blinded* the minds of unbelievers, so that they cannot see the light of the gospel that displays the glory of Christ, who is the image of God.

  2 Corinthians 4:4, emphasis added

- The mountain we are trying to climb is where God resides, His holy place.

  Who may ascend the mountain of the LORD? Who may stand in his holy place?

  Psalm 24:3

- The snake is a representation of Satan. Think Adam and Eve in Genesis:

  > Now the serpent was more crafty than any of the wild animals the LORD God had made. He said to the woman, "Did God really say, 'You must not eat from any tree in the garden'?"
  >
  > Genesis 3:1

- Just as the snake chased us in Tristan's dream, Satan chases us, looking for ways to attack us.

  > Be alert and of sober mind. Your enemy the devil prowls around like a roaring lion looking for someone to devour.
  >
  > 1 Peter 5:8

- My husband, as head of our family, destroys the enemy by praying the sinner's prayer with our son.

  > "I have given you authority to trample on snakes and scorpions and to overcome all the power of the enemy; nothing will harm you."
  >
  > Luke 10:19

- Tristan's vision is restored once he receives true salvation.

  > He replied, "Whether he is a sinner or not, I don't know. One thing I do know. I was blind but now I see!"
  >
  > John 9:25

- The three of us can now receive God's salvation and promises, unhindered by Satan:

  > In fact, this is love for God: to keep his commands. And his commands are not burdensome, for everyone born of God overcomes the world. This is the victory that

has overcome the world, even our faith. Who is it that overcomes the world? Only the one who believes that Jesus is the Son of God.

1 John 5:3–5

All this from the dream of a first-grader.

Tristan could not have made that up. He would not have known the significance of all of those symbols. God spoke to him through a dream as a sign to all of us of his new faith. Best of all, God saw my worried mama heart and cared enough to assure me that I had made the right choice in praying for salvation with my son. He did not have to do that. God has every right to expect me to believe without signs or visions. Mostly as a heartfelt gift to me had He given my son that dream.

Check Your Pulse

1. What do you believe about spiritual dreams?
2. God wants your heart to be eager to receive spiritual dreams. Is anything holding you back from receiving? Skepticism? Fear? Past experiences?
3. Take time to research different biblical instances of God using dreams to speak to His people. What stands out to you?
4. Given the opportunity to experience a spiritual dream, would you say yes? Why or why not?
5. If you feel prompted, pray for a spiritual dream this very night. As soon as you wake up, write down as much of the dream as possible and ask God to help you understand it.

fourteen

Best of Both Worlds

Kansas City is my home. I grew up in Kansas. I became a wife and mother in Missouri.

Kansas City is unusual, because it spans both states. Kansas City brought my two worlds together: the rural Kansas land I loved and the city streets I walked in Missouri.

I rooted for the Kansas City Royals baseball team year after year, even when they did not win. In a sea of blue, I turned out with hundreds of thousands of other fans to cheer them on to the World Series. Growing up, every special occasion was spent on the Plaza, a historic shopping district filled with award-winning restaurants and high-end specialty stores. My basketball team is the Kansas Jayhawks. My favorite movie is *The Wizard of Oz*, and I can name every hometown celebrity that hails from either Kansas or Missouri.

When I moved to Texas, I held on to my Kansas City identity tightly.

Texas was dead and brown. The trees were not trees; they were more like overgrown shrubs. It was hot. The mosquitoes were giant-sized. Everyone drove a pickup truck and knew about the local rodeo. The clothing shops were filled with fringed jackets and turquoise jewelry. Nothing looked like me or felt like me.

I wanted my tall trees, four seasons and stylish stores, pretty please. I refused to call myself a Texan. I would explain, "I just moved here. I am from Kansas City."

That line stops working well when you have lived in a state for a year. Then two. When was I going to drop my old identity and pick up my new one?

My friend Kate came to visit me in my new town. I complained to her the entire time. "Can you believe how many trucks there are on the roads here? Half these people don't even live on a ranch. Why do they need a truck? . . . I just don't fit in. No one here dresses like me or talks like me. I miss you and my old friends."

I complained about the smallest details. "The parks don't even have grass. They are basically dirt and rock. How is a kid going to play on that? Don't get me started on the school district, the city planners or the lack of code enforcement everywhere you look."

God finally calmed me down. He convinced me that I had better make myself comfortable, because I was not going to be leaving Texas anytime soon. I might as well accept my fate and learn to love my new home.

I reluctantly started counting my blessings. My house was a dream come true, an amazing Victorian beauty on a beautiful corner lot only blocks away from the historic downtown. While the trees in the rest of our area were sad and small, my yard had giant trees that flowered in the spring. Come to think of it, the people here were friendly and caring, and I could not think of anyone I had met who was not kind. Even though I did not care for the clothing in some of the local shops, I did love the fact that we had a strong local business community.

Wait a second. Do I actually like Texas?

I opened my heart up more to being a "local" with each passing day. By the time Kate visited me the following year, my heart had completely changed. She could tell right away.

"I am not sure why, but I remember not loving this town the last time I visited you. Now I think it is so cute!" she said. This showed me that my words the previous year must have been pretty nasty to affect how she viewed an entire city. What a shame.

I wish I had not waited so long to love where God had brought me, but I had invested my whole heart in Kansas City, having planted two churches there. I had prayed earnestly for my neighbors to know Christ, walking each block and pleading with God to open doors to share His love with my city. I loved its culture, schools and arts district. Its people were my people, and I felt such a sense of belonging there. If I fully embraced my new location, I worried that I might forget the old and all the years I had invested would have been a waste. I was scared to let go of the past.

That is how fear stifles our progress and strangles our dreams. But boldness unlocks our full potential. God showed me that by embracing the new place, I was enhancing the old one, not destroying it.

Spirit and Truth

It was time for another date for God and me. I was walking on a beautiful trail that wound through trees and past dusty rocks and cacti. My eyes were peeled for what God might be wanting to reveal to me. Around a curve, my heart jumped.

Stop, I heard the Spirit say, so I did. I felt a nudge to enter the woods. My adventurous side was excited to discover whatever might lie behind those trees. Pressing branches up and away, I ducked under pine needles and climbed over dead sticks into a dry creek bed.

Yes, this felt like where I was supposed to go. I knew God was going to speak to me in this place. I glanced around, wondering when a rare white fox would cross my path or an angel would descend from heaven to give me a message.

That would have to wait for another day, because today God was showing me a tree. In front of me was a gigantic live oak tree, its branches opening out far and wide like a giant extended hand, palm up, branches reaching like fingers into the sky.

It was by far the largest tree in the woods.

My eyes traced the ground surrounding the tree. The roots of this beast went deep. Two small streams had etched out paths flanking each side, and they merged as one directly in front of the tree. It was positioned right where the two streams came together to form a larger, stronger body of water.

You are this tree, Erica.

That's a new one, God.

Verses downloaded into my brain at lightning speed:

Blessed is the one who does not walk in step with the wicked or stand in the way that sinners take or sit in the company of mockers, but whose delight is in the law of the LORD, and who meditates on his law day and night. That person is like a tree planted by streams of water, which yields its fruit in season and whose leaf does not wither—whatever they do prospers.

Psalm 1:1–3

I loved those verses.

Erica, look at the other trees next to the two streams.

These trees looked nothing like my tree. Their roots had been drawn toward the side where the water flowed, causing the trees to lean crookedly over to one side. The flowing streams had eroded the banks and exposed their roots to the elements. Their branches overhead were entangled with each other in a fight for sunlight and survival. They were puny and struggling to survive.

But the Erica tree was balanced and healthy-looking.

Then more truth came, something I will never forget. God said, "One stream is Spirit. The other stream is Truth. Trees that are fed by only one will never reach their potential because they are always unbalanced and lacking. You, Erica, are now being fed by both streams, and your tree will be the biggest as a result."

My whole life I had been in the stream of Truth. Reading the Bible, memorizing Scripture, poring over commentaries and going to Bible college. I read and obeyed. Obeyed and read more. One stream flowed full force into my heart.

Now I had finally embraced the Spirit, and the uncontainable power of God in supernatural occurrences and unexplainable miracles. I had submerged myself in that stream and embraced all I tested and tried in those waters.

Now there were two streams feeding my soul: Spirit and Truth. This matched what Jesus said:

> Yet a time is coming and has now come when the true worshipers will worship the Father in the Spirit and in truth, for they are the kind of worshipers the Father seeks.
>
> John 4:23

I had never understood this statement before. People would say it when referred to an outpouring of charismatic power in worship settings. "We need the Spirit, but we gotta have the Truth." Did they mean that the Spirit and the Truth were two different things? How can God be divided? Did they mean they worshiped by reading the Bible and singing to music?

Now I understood. Spirit and Truth are like peanut butter and jelly—always better together. It had never been about one or the other. It has always been about both! God is equal parts strength and vulnerability, big-picture and small-detail, structured and free-flowing. He is all things good and holy and pure; He cannot be formulated or divided.

The two working together create a bigger story of the greatness of God. Far from being divided, our love gets multiplied. We can love the Spirit of God and His Truth, both. He encompasses it all. Why would His followers want to encounter Him any other way?

And seeking the Spirit does not mean abandoning the Truth, just as my embracing Texas did not mean throwing away my Kansas upbringing. Our value and identity are found in both, together.

Team Player

I used to love dodgeball.

We played it in school gym class. The gym teacher placed plastic-covered foam balls on the long line down the center of the basketball court. That line divided the room in half, one side versus the other. When the teacher blew the whistle, you ran as fast as you could to grab one of the balls and throw it at the other team. Your goal was to hit someone on the opposing team with your airborne ball. If you did, that player was out of the game and they had to sit along the gym wall until the game was over. Unless . . . (I love when a game has loopholes.) You could keep from being counted out if you caught the ball that was thrown at you. Then the person who threw the ball was "out" instead of you. Catching the ball was also like bringing a teammate back to life. If you caught the ball, you could choose someone from your team sitting along the wall to join you back in the game. The exhilaration of getting your buddy back in the game was the best. The winning team was the one that got every kid on the opposing team out.

The game's intensity grows when there are only a few kids left standing. Balls are flying; bodies are dodging; kids are desperately trying to catch everything thrown their way. With each ball caught, another teammate could come back into the fray to help, and the more people standing, the more likely that team would win.

Once I got older, I stopped enjoying dodgeball because the boys in my classroom grew things called "muscles." They thought it was hilarious to peg girls as hard as they could in the face to tag them out. I am still not sure why our gym teacher did not stop the madness.

Jesus Dodgeball

I believe if Jesus had walked into my school gym, He would have loved to play dodgeball with us. With His good sense of fun, I think it would appeal to Him. And His perfection would probably allow Him a few extra wins. I also know that Jesus would have never smacked me in the face with that stupid ball.

He loves to play and laugh, and He also loves it when His children work together to win. He loves our comradery and strategy-building. He made us for friendship and community, so seeing us all work together must make His heart happy. Jesus spent time with His friends when He was on earth. He ate with them and shared stories with them. He enjoyed them personally, and the feeling was mutual.

Two sisters, Mary and Martha, who lived in Bethany along with their brother Lazarus, were among those who loved Him and who embraced His teaching. They spent time together when Jesus was in town.

One day, Lazarus got very sick. Jesus was away somewhere, so the women sent an urgent message to Him. These women had seen Jesus heal the sick. They knew that He could heal Lazarus with a touch and that if He came, they would have nothing to worry about. However, Jesus did not come as soon as He was summoned. He assured the messenger that Lazarus would not die and then He stayed right where He was for another two days before heading to Bethany. When finally He arrived, Lazarus had been dead four days. Four days. The book of John tells the rest of the story:

> Jesus, once more deeply moved, came to the tomb. It was a cave with a stone laid across the entrance. "Take away the stone," he said.
>
> "But, Lord," said Martha, the sister of the dead man, "by this time there is a bad odor, for he has been there four days."
>
> Then Jesus said, "Did I not tell you that if you believe, you will see the glory of God?" So they took away the stone. Then Jesus looked up and said, "Father, I thank you that you have heard me. I knew that you always hear me, but I said this for the benefit of the people standing here, that they may believe that you sent me."
>
> When he had said this, Jesus called in a loud voice, "Lazarus, come out!" The dead man came out, his hands and feet wrapped with strips of linen, and a cloth around his face.
>
> Jesus said to them, "Take off the grave clothes and let him go."
>
> John 11:38–44

This is why I say that Jesus is the ultimate Comeback Kid. There He was, facing a wall of opposition, his teammates lined against the gym wall. He stared death in the eye and caught the ball thrown at Him. He called Lazarus back onto the court and they won. Jesus is in the game of resurrecting His people. Though we may be sitting on the sidelines, facing stinging rejection, He calls us to play and He makes it possible. He wants us on the court with Him. After all, the more He has on His team, the better.

You are on His team. You are called to play a vital role in His Kingdom. He knows it will not always be fun, but you have to try. You need to rush the line and grab the ball. Run, jump, grab, throw. Count on your teammates to have your back, and you protect theirs, as well. Being bold means taking risks and getting knocked down. You can be sure that Jesus will not leave you down. He will call out something in you that makes you come alive, just as He did for Lazarus.

Time to Grow Up

Today I want to invite you to write your own story as you walk into bold faith. There is nothing more gratifying than a life surrendered completely to God, in which you trust Him to show you new and wonderful truths. Of course you have common sense (at least I hope you do), and you may hesitate sometimes. It is fine to wonder and ask questions before you take risks. In fact, God loves it when you do. You do not have to worry about messing up, because He is right beside you and He will never let you fall.

Bold faith looks different for everyone. If you ground yourself through constant prayer, there is no telling how God will use you. Your journey will look nothing like mine. Whatever happens, you can be sure that it will be a perfect fit for you.

Bold faith does not always mean saying a lot. It may mean holding your tongue when you want to speak in order to allow God to speak to the other person's heart directly. Bold faith may mean praying out loud in your small group for the first time. Boldness for you may entail merely believing that you are hearing God's often-subtle voice. Every one of these examples represents a genuine movement of God; do not discount such things.

With growth come growing pains. Like a lanky teen learning to control his big feet and long arms, you will not always get the steps right. You will trip and fall and skin your knee. As you step out, learning to operate in God's power, you will need correction and redirection. These are not bad for you.

If you are using your gifts in a corporate setting, have a talk with whoever is in charge. Let that person know how God has been growing you, and then submit to the authority God has given them in that setting.

Honor the process your church follows for the expression of the gifts. Put yourself under the authority of those in charge and use your gift in an orderly fashion. Honor the people around you. When they mess up, and they will, cover them in grace and love. Encourage them to try again. If God tells you to share your dream, share your dream. If He prompts you to pray over someone, ask for their permission. If your offer is rejected or not well received, that is okay. God will teach you as you grow; there is no shame in being a learner.

I do not know the details of your background and I will never be able to walk in your shoes. I do not know if you were raised Baptist or Pentecostal, Methodist or Presbyterian, but regardless, if you are one of His own, God has a bold faith waiting for you. He wants to move mountains through you, but you must step out in faith.

Remember the two streams, Spirit and Truth. If up to now you have only been led by the Spirit in prayer, how about trying a new way of praying—praying through the Bible? If you cannot pray without the Bible in your hand, try simply sitting quietly and allowing the Holy Spirit to speak to you without the direction of those red letters. Unless you are living in both streams, you will struggle and miss out on much growth.

Are you praying bold prayers? If so, God will begin to awaken more gifts in you. He will increase what He has already given you.

My story is not your story, but I hope it gives you the courage you need to go the distance in your faith. Do not let your faith stagnate as you age. Do not be one of those believers who never grows or changes, held back by fear or voices from your past. Listen to Jesus' voice as He calls you out from death into life. Now is your time. This is your chance to be all He created you to be. Don't back down. Don't sit it out. Don't stop believing.

Be bold.

Be brave.

Be you.

My name is **Erica Willis** and I love how God surprises me. I find my best conversations sitting across from a friend with a hot cup of coffee. It is my passion to see others embrace the life God has designed for them uniquely, and to challenge them to run their race well.

Even after having been in church ministry over twenty years, I had never seen a move of God like I read about in the Bible. I was not going to be satisfied until I witnessed God's miracles and healing with my own eyes, so I started praying for break-through to happen. I prayed every morning at 5:00 a.m. Thus, my worldwide prayer ministry, #theFives, was born, providing early-morning accountability for me and hundreds of praying friends. Every morning, we plead for God to show up in big ways. Man, does He deliver! Today #theFives spans all time zones in the United States, has participants in more than five countries and grows more every session. Praying has never been cooler. I share my journey online at BelieveBoldy.com and you can find me on Twitter, Instagram and Facebook @Believe Boldly.

I currently live in Texas and still have not adapted to the sugar levels in the tea, but I am never one to back down from a challenge. My heart beats for the local church, having planted two church locations in the Kansas City area, and having served as worship director, children's pastor and wherever else God has called me. I am currently serving in women's ministry, the area of the church I had vowed never to touch, but now I love. I could go on, but that story is for another book.

My children, Tristan and Reese, are the greatest joys of my life and teach me more about the unconditional love of God every day. I would do anything for them, even buy them a French bulldog named River. I am married to Joey, the love of my life, and I would not be the woman I am today without his integrity, passion and limitless support of all I dream to accomplish. As we like to say, "Teamwork makes the dream work," and it has never been truer than with him by my side.